THE FAMILY CFO

HOW BUSINESS FAMILIES, HNIS & GLOBAL INDIANS CAN MOVE FROM SCATTERED WEALTH TO GOVERNED WEALTH

VICTOR TANDY

Made with ♥ on the Notion Press Platform
www.notionpress.com

To you—

the founder, steward, spouse, successor or family member carrying the responsibility of what has been built.

May this book help you bring greater order to your wealth, confidence to your decisions, and continuity to the generations that follow.

Contents

Contents

Disclaimer

This book has been written for educational and informational purposes. It presents a framework for financial organisation, wealth governance, coordination, documentation, review discipline and family continuity. It is not intended to provide, and should not be interpreted as providing, personalised investment advice, legal advice, tax advice, accounting advice, estate-planning advice, insurance advice or any other regulated professional service.

Nothing in this book should be understood as a recommendation to buy, sell, hold, replace or avoid any security, mutual fund scheme, portfolio management service, alternative investment fund, bond, insurance policy, loan, real-estate asset or other financial product. The book does not prescribe asset-allocation percentages, model portfolios, target returns or expected returns, and it does not guarantee any financial outcome.

The expression "Family CFO" is used in this book as a descriptive wealth-governance and coordination model. It is not presented as a statutory, regulatory or professional designation. A Family CFO, as described here, helps a family organise financial information, establish reporting and review systems, coordinate specialists, track decisions and actions, improve documentation and prepare for continuity. The role does not replace the work of appropriately registered, licensed or qualified professionals.

Investment recommendations, securities advice and other regulated financial activities should be obtained from professionals holding the registrations required for the relevant service. Legal documents and legal opinions should be prepared or provided by qualified legal professionals. Taxation, accounting, residency, cross-border reporting, remittance, succession and estate matters should be reviewed with appropriately qualified professionals in each relevant jurisdiction. Insurance-related decisions should be undertaken with due consideration of policy terms, disclosures, exclusions and the assistance of appropriately licensed professionals.

Laws, regulations, tax provisions, product rules and institutional processes may change. The reader should not rely on any general statement in this book as a substitute for current professional verification. Illustrations and composite examples are included only to explain governance principles. They do not represent recommendations, promises, forecasts or a complete analysis of any person's circumstances.

Every family's situation is different. Before implementing any financial, legal, tax, estate, insurance or business-continuity decision, the reader should obtain advice appropriate to the family's facts, objectives, jurisdiction and regulatory context.

The author and publisher have taken reasonable care in preparing this material. However, they accept no responsibility for any loss, damage, claim, liability or consequence arising from reliance upon, or action taken on the basis of, the information contained in this book.

Author's Note

Successful families rarely become financially disorganised because they do not care about money. More often, the opposite is true. They work hard, make decisions, acquire assets, build businesses, support relatives, appoint professionals and respond to opportunities as they arise. Over time, each decision may be reasonable on its own. The difficulty appears when no single system connects them.

A property may be held in one name, a business interest in another and a financial account in a third. One professional understands taxation, another understands legal documentation, a banker knows the operating accounts and a distributor knows a portion of the investments. Important documents may exist, but not in one place. A spouse may know the broad picture without knowing the details. The founder may carry most of the family's financial memory personally.

This book grew from a simple observation: as wealth becomes more substantial, the family's central financial question changes. It is no longer only, "Where should we invest?" It becomes, "How is everything connected, who is responsible, what remains unresolved, and will the system continue to work when circumstances change?"

The Family CFO is my answer to that question—not as another product, and not as a substitute for the family's existing professionals. It is a way of thinking about wealth as a governed system. It brings together visibility, ownership, risk, liquidity, documentation, decision-making, professional coordination and continuity.

My purpose is not to tell families what to buy. It is to help them see why a collection of individually sensible decisions may still produce a fragmented financial life. A chartered accountant, lawyer, banker, mutual fund distributor, registered investment adviser, insurance professional and business consultant may all contribute essential expertise. Yet expertise does not automatically create coordination. Someone must still maintain the consolidated picture, clarify responsibilities and ensure that important actions move from discussion to completion.

The families I have in mind are not defined only by net worth. They are business owners whose personal and business finances overlap; Global Indians whose assets and obligations cross borders; senior professionals with little time to administer growing complexity; and families preparing to transfer responsibility from one generation to another.

You will not find market forecasts, model portfolios or promises of superior returns in these pages. You will find questions that are often postponed because they appear administrative: What do we own? In whose name? Against which obligations? Where are the documents? Who can act if the principal decision-maker is unavailable? Which professional is responsible for the next step? When was the matter last reviewed?

These are not minor questions. They determine whether wealth remains understandable and usable when the family needs it most.

I hope this book gives you a sharper vocabulary for discussing your family's financial life and a practical framework for organising the work ahead. Wealth deserves more than accumulation. It deserves stewardship.

Prologue

The Question No One Had Asked

The following is a composite illustration reflecting patterns commonly seen across affluent and business families.

The family had never considered itself financially disorganised.

The business was successful. There were properties, investments, insurance policies, several bank accounts and a team of professionals that included a chartered accountant, lawyer, banker and insurance specialist.

Everything appeared to be in place.

Then the family patriarch faced a medical emergency and was advised to step away from work for several weeks.

His temporary absence exposed a problem no one had previously noticed.

A banker asked for account information that no one could immediately locate. An insurance premium notice arrived, but the family was unsure who owned the policy or where the full records were kept. Property documents were believed to be in one of several cupboards. Certain investments appeared across different statements, but no consolidated record explained their purpose, ownership or intended use.

A will was thought to exist.

No one knew where the latest version was.

By the end of the week, files, passwords, statements and handwritten notes were spread across the dining table. Each family member knew something. No one knew everything.

The family did not lack wealth.

It lacked a reliable way to see and coordinate that wealth.

For years, the system had depended on one person's memory. He knew which professional to call, why certain decisions had been made, where important documents were kept and which obligations remained unresolved.

As long as he was available, the weakness remained invisible.

His absence did not create the disorder. It revealed it.

The family had accumulated assets, but not a complete asset register. It had professional relationships, but no one coordinating them. It had documents, but no dependable document map. It had succession intentions, but limited continuity of financial knowledge.

No single investment or financial product could solve this problem.

What the family needed was a system—one that brought together assets, liabilities, ownership, documents, risks, professionals and decisions into a single, governed view.

That need leads to the central question of this book:

When wealth is spread across people, businesses, assets, documents and professionals, who is responsible for looking at the whole picture?

The Question Changes After Wealth Is Created

In the early stage of financial life, money is usually visible. Income arrives in one or two accounts. Expenses are familiar. A small number of investments can be remembered without a dashboard. The individual who earns the money often makes most of the decisions and knows where the documents are kept.

Success changes this.

A business grows. Properties are acquired at different times and for different purposes. Bank accounts multiply. Investments are made through more than one institution. Loans and guarantees enter the picture. Family members begin living in different cities or countries. Tax, legal, banking, insurance and investment professionals become involved. The family's financial life expands not only in value, but also in the number of relationships, obligations and decisions that must be coordinated.

Most families respond to this growth by adding specialists. That is often necessary. Yet the addition of expertise does not automatically create a unified financial system. Each professional usually works within a defined mandate. The accountant may focus on reporting and taxation. The lawyer may address a document or transaction. The banker may understand the accounts maintained with one institution. A distributor or registered adviser may work with a particular part of the financial assets. The family may receive sound inputs from all of them and still lack a consolidated view.

That is the central problem of this book: scattered wealth without unified governance.

The word "scattered" does not necessarily mean careless. It can describe a family in which every asset is legitimate, every professional is competent and every decision had a reasonable explanation at the time it was made. The scattering occurs because the decisions were made at different moments, for different needs, by different people, through different entities and under changing circumstances.

The result may remain invisible for years. Normal life allows the founder to bridge gaps through memory and personal involvement. A missing document can be found after a few telephone calls. An unclear ownership issue can be deferred. An account that nobody else understands can continue to operate because the principal decision-maker is available. The system appears to work because one person repeatedly compensates for its weaknesses.

Then circumstances change.

The founder becomes ill, travels for an extended period or begins withdrawing from day-to-day responsibility. A family member moves abroad. A business restructures. A marriage, birth, death or dispute changes the ownership context. A liquidity requirement emerges at an inconvenient time. A professional asks for information that no one has consolidated. A spouse or child must suddenly understand decisions that were never documented.

At that point, the family may discover that it possesses wealth but not an operating system for that wealth.

Beyond the Question of Returns

Financial conversations are often organised around products and performance. Which investment should be selected? Which asset has produced the highest return? Which opportunity should be acted upon? These questions matter, but they are downstream questions. Before a family decides what to implement, it should be able to answer a more fundamental set of questions.

What is the purpose of the money? Who owns it? Who depends upon it? What obligations compete for it? When may it be required? What risks surround the decision? Who has the authority to act? Which professional must be consulted? What records will be maintained? When will the decision be reviewed?

These are governance questions.

Governance does not mean bureaucracy for its own sake. It means that visibility, responsibility, authority, documentation and review are deliberately assigned. It allows the family to understand not merely what it owns, but how the different parts of its financial life affect one another.

A family may have a valuable business and still face personal liquidity stress. It may have several insurance policies and still be unable to explain which risk each policy was intended to address. It may have completed nominations but not reviewed the legal implications of ownership and succession. It may have appointed multiple professionals but not identified who is responsible for coordinating a decision that crosses professional boundaries.

The objective is not to centralise every decision in one person. The objective is to create a structure in which the right people have the right information, responsibilities are clear, important matters are documented and the family can continue operating through change.

The Family CFO Idea

In a company, the chief financial officer does not personally perform every specialised task. Auditors, tax experts, lawyers, bankers, treasury teams and department heads may all contribute. The CFO's value lies partly in maintaining the integrated financial picture: the reports, obligations, risks, decisions, priorities and follow-through.

Families with growing complexity often need a comparable organising function. This book calls that function the Family CFO.

The Family CFO described here is not a regulatory title and does not replace licensed or qualified professionals. It is a governance and coordination model. Its purpose is to help the family create visibility, connect specialist inputs, maintain decision records, identify unresolved actions, establish a review rhythm and prepare for continuity.

The role may be performed in different ways. In a relatively simple family, one disciplined family member may maintain the system with periodic professional support. In a more complex family, the work may require a dedicated external coordinator or an internal family-office function. The appropriate form depends upon complexity, not prestige.

The central principle remains the same: someone must own the consolidated view.

The Six Engines

The framework developed in this book organises family wealth into six connected engines.

The Core Engine establishes visibility: assets, liabilities, ownership, entities, documents, contacts and decision records. The Income Engine governs the movement of money into and through the family. The Growth Engine addresses the discipline surrounding long-term wealth-building decisions. The Security Engine maps the risks that may destabilise the family or business. The Liquidity Engine protects access to resources when timing matters. The Legacy Engine prepares ownership, knowledge and responsibility to continue beyond the first generation.

The engines are not products. They are areas of governance. Their purpose is to help a family identify what must be visible, who must be involved, what must be documented and how matters should be reviewed.

This book begins with the problem of disorganisation and fragmentation. It then introduces the shift from product-led thinking to governance-led thinking, defines the Family CFO and presents the Family Wealth Operating System. The six engines are examined individually before the framework is applied to Global Indian families, periodic reviews and the decision of whether a dedicated Family CFO arrangement is necessary.

The appendices convert the concepts into practical tools: a governance scorecard, a dashboard template, an emergency-file checklist, questions for financial professionals and a 90-day implementation roadmap.

A Different Measure of Financial Strength

Net worth is an important measure, but it is incomplete. A family's financial strength also depends upon whether its wealth is understandable, accessible and capable of surviving change.

Can the family produce a reliable consolidated view without weeks of effort? Are ownership and obligations clear? Do the relevant people know where documents are kept? Can the spouse or next generation continue essential financial operations? Are specialist recommendations connected to the family's wider position? Are decisions recorded, assigned and reviewed?

The purpose of these questions is not to create anxiety. It is to reveal where success may have outgrown its supporting systems.

The next stage of wealth is not defined only by acquiring more. It is defined by governing what has already been created.

Welcome to the Family CFO way of thinking.

I

Part I — The Problem: Wealth Without Governance

Wealth often becomes scattered before the family recognises that a system is missing. The first three chapters examine the difference between accumulation and organisation, the hidden cost of fragmentation and the limits of relying upon several specialists without one consolidated view.

II

CHAPTER 1: Rich Is Not the Same as Organised

A family can look financially impressive from the outside and remain surprisingly difficult to understand from within.

There may be a successful operating business, several properties, substantial bank balances, investments accumulated over many years and a network of respected professionals. The family may enjoy a high standard of living and meet every visible obligation. Yet a simple request for a consolidated picture can trigger days of searching, telephone calls and approximations.

How many assets does the family own? In whose names are they held? Which liabilities or guarantees relate to them? Where are the original documents? What income does each asset produce? Which accounts are active? Which nominations are current? What must be renewed this year? Who can operate essential accounts if the principal decision-maker is unavailable?

The inability to answer these questions promptly does not mean the family is not wealthy. It means wealth and organisation have developed at different speeds.

Accumulation Is Not Organisation

Asset accumulation is usually event-driven. A business owner purchases a property when a good opportunity appears. A senior executive begins an investment while working with a particular institution. A family opens an account to meet an immediate need. An insurance policy is taken when a loan is sanctioned or a child is born. A new entity is created for a commercial purpose. A family member moves abroad and establishes a second financial life in another jurisdiction.

Each action may be sensible. The organisational problem arises because the information surrounding the action is rarely integrated into one dependable system.

The purchase document may remain with the lawyer who handled the transaction. The loan details may sit in a separate email account. The spouse may know about the property but not the financing arrangement. The accountant may record the asset for tax purposes but may not maintain the family's operational information. A nomination may have been completed years earlier and never reviewed. The reason for the purchase may exist only in the founder's memory.

Accumulation answers the question, "What have we acquired?"

Organisation answers a broader set of questions: "What exactly do we own, through whom, against what obligations, for what purpose, with which records and under whose responsibility?"

These are different capabilities.

A family may be excellent at identifying opportunities and still be weak at maintaining records. It may negotiate transactions skilfully and still have no unified ownership map. It may earn high returns from parts of its wealth while being unable to explain the purpose of other holdings. Financial success does not automatically produce administrative discipline.

Complexity Arrives Quietly

Financial disorganisation rarely appears as one dramatic failure. It develops in layers.

The first layer is usually manageable. One person knows the accounts, remembers the fixed deposits, keeps the property papers and speaks to the accountant. When another asset is added, that person still manages. When the family appoints another banker or purchases a second property, the system stretches but continues to function.

Over time, the family becomes dependent upon memory. Information is distributed across mobile phones, email inboxes, paper files, messaging applications and professional offices. Some records are current; others reflect a position from several years ago. Similar assets may be described differently by different institutions. The same family member may be listed under several versions of a name. Liabilities may be known in total but not mapped to specific assets or entities.

During normal periods, these imperfections appear harmless. The person at the centre of the system answers questions as they arise. Gaps are resolved through effort. A missing statement is downloaded. A professional is called. A document is found eventually.

The system therefore seems more organised than it is. What appears to be a process may actually be one individual repeatedly compensating for the absence of a process.

This is why successful people can underestimate financial disorganisation. They are accustomed to solving problems. Their competence conceals the fragility of the structure.

The Observable Signs

A family does not need a sophisticated audit to identify early signs of disorganisation. The symptoms are usually familiar.

Information about assets is maintained in several versions, none of which is treated as final. The value of the family's wealth can be estimated, but not reconciled. Documents are available, but their location is known only to one person. Accounts continue to exist because nobody has decided whether they are still required. Investments are remembered by institution rather than by purpose. Property ownership is known broadly, while co-ownership percentages, encumbrances or supporting records require further checking.

Liabilities are often less visible than assets. A family may remember the principal loans but overlook guarantees, overdrafts, business obligations or commitments made to relatives. Personal and business resources may be used interchangeably without a clear record of the resulting exposure.

Responsibility may also be unclear. The family assumes the accountant is monitoring one matter, the banker believes the family will initiate it, and the family expects the lawyer to follow up. No one is negligent; no one has been clearly assigned ownership.

Another sign is the absence of a reliable date. When was the information last updated? When were nominations reviewed? When was the family's liquidity position examined? When was the will compared with current ownership? A document that was accurate five years ago can create a false sense of security today.

Organisation is not proven by the existence of information. It is proven by the family's ability to retrieve, explain and update that information.

A Family That Knew Its Wealth but Not Its Structure

Consider an illustrative family led by a first-generation entrepreneur, whom we will call Mr Sen.

Over three decades, Mr Sen built a profitable manufacturing business. The family owned its home, two commercial properties, agricultural land inherited from the previous generation and a small portfolio of financial assets. One child worked in the business. The other lived overseas. The family had a chartered accountant, a lawyer, two banking relationships and several insurance and investment contacts.

Mr Sen could estimate the family's net worth with confidence. But when the family attempted to prepare a consolidated record, the apparent simplicity disappeared.

One commercial property was owned personally but used by the company. The loan taken against it had been repaid, although the closure documents had not been placed with the title papers. The inherited land remained in names that did not reflect the present family structure. One investment account used an old address. The overseas child was a nominee in some accounts but not others. Several policies existed, but no single record described their purpose, ownership, beneficiaries or renewal status. A personal guarantee given years earlier had not been included in the family's liability summary.

None of these facts proved that a loss had occurred. The family remained prosperous. The problem was that its prosperity could not be expressed as one reliable operating picture.

The exercise also revealed a deeper dependence. Mr Sen understood why each arrangement existed. Other family members knew fragments. The system was organised in his mind, not in a form the family could independently use.

That distinction matters. Wealth held by a family should not require one person's continuous presence merely to remain understandable.

Organisation Before Sophistication

Affluent families are often encouraged to consider increasingly sophisticated opportunities. Yet sophistication cannot compensate for a weak foundation.

Before adding another structure, account, product or professional relationship, the family should know whether its existing financial life is visible and current. A consolidated asset list will not answer every question, but it will reveal what questions remain. An ownership map will not resolve legal issues, but it will show where legal verification is needed. A document register will not replace the documents, but it will identify what exists, where it is kept and who may access it.

Organisation also improves the quality of professional conversations. A specialist who receives accurate, consolidated information can understand the context more quickly. The family can distinguish facts from assumptions. Decisions can be recorded against a clear starting position.

This does not require the family to create excessive paperwork. The goal is not to document every minor transaction. It is to ensure that material assets, obligations, relationships and decisions can be understood without reconstructing the family's financial history each time a question arises.

A More Useful Question

The question "How much are we worth?" remains important. It provides a measure of scale and progress. But it does not reveal whether the family is financially prepared.

A more useful set of questions is harder and more practical.

Can we produce a current consolidated view? Can we identify the legal and beneficial ownership of important assets? Can we connect liabilities and guarantees to the assets, businesses or decisions that created them? Can another responsible family member find the essential records? Can our professionals work from the same underlying information? Can the system continue if the person who currently holds the knowledge is unavailable?

These questions move the family from the appearance of wealth to the organisation of wealth.

Being rich describes what the family has accumulated. Being organised describes whether that wealth can be seen, explained, accessed and carried forward.

III

CHAPTER 2: The Hidden Cost of Scattered Wealth

The most expensive weaknesses in a family's financial life do not always appear as a fee, penalty or investment loss. Some appear as delay. Others appear as duplicated effort, missed information, forced decisions or the gradual exhaustion of the person expected to remember everything.

These costs are difficult to measure because the family experiences them separately. A document search consumes two hours. A renewal is missed. A decision is postponed until figures are reconciled. Two professionals request the same information in different formats. An account remains open because nobody is certain why it exists. A family member avoids asking questions because the answers are complicated.

No single event appears serious enough to justify redesigning the system. Together, however, they create what may be called a complexity tax: the recurring cost of operating wealth without a unified structure.

The Price of Reconstructing the Picture

When information is scattered, every important decision begins with reconstruction.

The family first has to determine what it owns, which version of the data is current, which documents are available and which professional has the relevant history. Only then can the actual question be addressed.

This process consumes more than administrative time. It delays judgement. A decision that should take a day may remain open for weeks because information arrives in stages. Each new fact changes the context. The family discusses the same subject repeatedly, but never from a complete starting point.

The burden often falls upon the founder or one financially involved family member. That person becomes the unofficial switchboard for every question. The accountant asks for records. The banker asks for a signature. The lawyer asks how an asset is held. The spouse asks whether funds are available for a planned commitment. The same individual answers each request separately and remains responsible for remembering what happened next.

Time is not merely lost; attention is fragmented. The family's most capable decision-maker may spend hours locating information that should have been available through a maintained system.

For business owners, this distraction has a particular cost. Time used to reconcile personal financial matters is time not used for customers, employees, strategy or rest. The wealth may have been created through disciplined enterprise, yet its administration gradually competes with the activity that created it.

Delay Changes the Quality of Decisions

A delayed decision is not always a neutral decision.

An insurance claim can become more difficult when records are incomplete. A legal document may remain outdated after a change in family circumstances. A loan closure may not be followed by the required release or record update. A large payment may be met from the most accessible source rather than the most appropriate source because the family has not reviewed its liquidity in advance.

The issue is not that every delay causes loss. The issue is that delay reduces the family's range of choices.

When a family has time, it can compare alternatives, consult specialists and organise documentation. When time has been consumed by confusion, it may accept the first workable answer. Urgency converts optionality into necessity.

This is one reason affluent families sometimes make surprisingly improvised decisions. The underlying wealth may be substantial, but the information required to use it intelligently is not available at the right moment.

Duplication and Leakage

Fragmented systems frequently produce duplicated work.

The same KYC records are collected by several people but never maintained in a shared, secure register. The same asset is valued differently in separate summaries. The family asks the accountant to prepare a report that partially duplicates information held by another professional. A banker creates a new arrangement without visibility into an existing one. Legal documents are reviewed one transaction at a time rather than against a complete ownership map.

Duplication appears harmless because each task has a purpose. The cost lies in repeatedly paying—in money, time or attention—to rediscover facts the family has already established.

Financial leakage can also occur in small, unremarkable forms. Charges continue on inactive accounts. Renewals are accepted without review because deadlines are missed. Refunds, maturity proceeds or receivables remain untracked. Guarantees stay on record after the associated obligation has changed. Idle balances accumulate in places no one monitors because each account is considered separately.

This chapter is not suggesting that every idle rupee should be deployed or that every account should be closed. Such decisions require context. The governance failure is the absence of a deliberate decision. An arrangement continues not because the family has chosen it, but because nobody has reviewed it.

Over years, unexamined arrangements can become expensive. More importantly, they make the family's financial position harder to explain.

The Human Cost of Institutional Memory

The most fragile financial system is one in which a single person acts as the database.

That person may know the passwords, document locations, bank managers, reasons behind investments, informal family commitments and history of professional advice. The family may regard this as efficiency: questions are answered quickly because the knowledgeable person is available.

But concentrated knowledge creates two kinds of risk.

The first is operational. If the individual is ill, unavailable, incapacitated or deceased, the family must reconstruct decisions without context. It may know that an asset exists but not why it was held. It may find a document without knowing whether it is current. It may contact a professional without knowing the scope of the relationship.

The second is relational. Other family members may feel excluded from financial decisions even when exclusion was never intended. The knowledgeable person may feel burdened and underappreciated. Spouses may avoid the subject because discussions become technical. Adult children may receive information only during emergencies, when there is little time to learn.

A system that depends entirely upon one person may work efficiently for that person and poorly for the family.

Good organisation does not require every family member to know every detail. It requires the right people to know that reliable information exists, where it is kept and how authority will operate when needed.

When Small Gaps Converge

Consider an illustrative family in which the principal earner, Mrs Mehra, managed a professional practice and most household financial matters. Her husband handled property maintenance but did not participate in banking or investment administration. Their adult children lived in other cities.

Over time, the family accumulated several accounts, two properties, insurance policies, practice-related liabilities and investments made through different institutions. Mrs Mehra maintained a personal spreadsheet, but it had not been updated for eighteen months. Some documents were stored at home, some in an office cabinet and others in email folders.

A sudden hospitalisation did not create a financial crisis. It created an information crisis.

The family needed to arrange a large payment, identify available funds and confirm policy procedures. The husband knew the bank names but not which account served which purpose. One child could access the spreadsheet but could not determine which figures were current. The insurance professional had policy information but not the family's wider liquidity position. The accountant knew the practice accounts but not all personal holdings.

No single gap was catastrophic. Together, they consumed critical time and forced the family to act with partial information.

After the emergency, the family's first reaction was to update the spreadsheet. That was necessary but incomplete. The deeper requirement was to decide who would maintain the consolidated record, where documents would be kept, how access would be granted and which matters would trigger a review.

The lesson was not that Mrs Mehra had managed badly. She had managed too much personally for too long.

Visible Costs and Invisible Costs

Families tend to scrutinise visible charges because they are easy to compare. An explicit fee invites examination. The invisible cost of fragmentation is rarely presented on a statement.

How much time does the family spend gathering information each year? How often are decisions postponed? How many professional hours are used to reconcile incomplete data? Which obligations remain open because ownership is unclear? How much stress is created when the spouse or next generation cannot independently understand the system?

These questions do not produce a precise figure, but they reveal an important principle: financial efficiency is not only about reducing expenses. It is also about reducing unnecessary complexity.

A well-governed family may still face difficult decisions, market uncertainty, legal processes and changing regulations. Organisation does not remove those realities. It prevents avoidable confusion from being added to them.

The Cost Appears at the Worst Time

Scattered wealth often seems manageable while the family has time, health and access to the principal decision-maker. The system is tested only when one of those advantages disappears.

That is why the greatest cost may remain hidden for years. It is not charged annually. It emerges during a transaction, illness, succession, dispute, relocation or liquidity need—precisely when the family has the least capacity to search, reconcile and debate.

The complexity tax is paid in fragments. Its full price is discovered when the family can least afford delay.

IV

CHAPTER 3: Why More Advisors Do Not Always Mean More Clarity

Affluent families often respond to complexity by appointing more specialists. This is usually sensible. Tax matters require tax expertise. Legal documents require lawyers. Banking, insurance, investments, business finance and cross-border matters each involve knowledge that one person should not be expected to possess.

The difficulty is not the presence of specialists. It is the assumption that specialists automatically create an integrated system.

A family can receive competent work from every professional and still remain unclear about its overall position. Each person may deliver exactly what was requested, while important questions fall between mandates.

Excellence Within a Limited View

Professional work is organised around scope.

A chartered accountant may focus on accounts, filings, tax positions and the records required for those responsibilities. A lawyer may be engaged for a property transaction, a will or a corporate matter. A banker may understand the products, facilities and mandates maintained with one institution. A mutual fund distributor or registered investment adviser may work with a defined portion of the financial assets. An insurance professional may maintain policy records and support servicing or claims.

Each perspective is valuable. None necessarily represents the family's complete financial life.

The accountant may know that a property exists because it appears in financial records, but may not know where the original title documents are stored. The lawyer may draft a will based on information provided at one point in time, but may not be informed when ownership later changes. The banker may understand available credit but not the family's contingent liabilities elsewhere. The investment professional may understand a portfolio without visibility into a large business exposure that affects the family's overall risk.

This is not professional failure. It is the natural consequence of specialised mandates.

The problem begins when the family assumes that because several professionals are involved, someone must be connecting the information.

Often, no one is.

Different Data, Different Timelines

Professionals also work with different versions of reality.

The accountant's data may reflect the previous financial year. The banker may work with the most recent account balances. The lawyer may rely upon ownership documents prepared years earlier. The family may discuss values using current estimates. An overseas professional may use classifications that differ from those used in India.

Even when each version is correct for its purpose, the differences can create confusion.

A family asks whether it has sufficient liquidity for a major commitment. The banker identifies available balances. The accountant points to upcoming tax payments. The business team expects funds to be retained for working capital. The investment professional notes that some assets may not be intended for near-term use. Each answer is reasonable. The decision remains unresolved because no one has assembled the answers into one family-level view.

Timelines create similar gaps. A legal review may occur when a document is signed. A tax review may occur at year-end. Insurance renewals follow policy dates. Investment reviews follow another calendar. The family's important decisions do not necessarily occur on any of those schedules.

Without a central review rhythm, the family operates through a series of professional appointments rather than one coordinated process.

The Space Between Mandates

The most consequential work often lies between professional categories.

Who confirms that ownership records used for the will match the current asset register? Who ensures that a change in business borrowing is reflected in the family risk map? Who records that an account opened for a temporary purpose should be reviewed after the purpose ends? Who follows up when one professional recommends that another professional examine an issue?

These tasks may not belong naturally to any specialist. They are coordination tasks.

When coordination is not assigned, families rely upon informal assumptions. The lawyer assumes the accountant will provide updated information. The accountant assumes the family will consult the lawyer.

The banker assumes authorised signatories have been considered elsewhere. The family assumes one of the professionals is monitoring the whole matter.

No one has acted improperly. Yet the action remains incomplete.

This is why adding another specialist may increase the number of inputs without increasing clarity. The family receives more information but still lacks ownership of the connections.

Opinions Are Not a Decision Framework

Successful people often seek second and third opinions. That can improve judgement. But several opinions do not automatically become a decision.

Each opinion may be based on a different question. One professional may optimise tax efficiency. Another may prioritise legal protection. A third may emphasise liquidity or ease of administration. The recommendations can appear contradictory when they are actually responding to different objectives.

The family needs a framework that clarifies which objectives matter, what constraints apply, who has authority and how trade-offs will be resolved.

For example, a structure that appears efficient from one perspective may create administrative complexity from another. A decision that improves short-term liquidity may affect long-term ownership or succession. A family cannot resolve these tensions merely by counting professional opinions. It must decide how the different considerations fit together.

A decision framework does not eliminate disagreement. It makes the basis of disagreement visible.

It also records the conclusion. Why was one path chosen? Which assumptions were accepted? What conditions would require the decision to be revisited? Who was responsible for implementation?

Without this record, the family may reopen the same debate months later with a different set of facts and no memory of the original reasoning.

The Orchestra Without a Conductor

An orchestra can contain exceptional musicians and still produce confusion if timing, sequence and interpretation are not coordinated.

The analogy should not be taken too far, but it captures an important point. Specialists do not lose their expertise when coordination is introduced. Their expertise becomes more useful because it is placed within a shared score.

For a family, the shared score is the consolidated financial picture: assets, ownership, liabilities, obligations, risks, documents, decisions and deadlines. Coordination establishes when each professional is required, what information must be shared and who is responsible for the next action.

The coordinating function does not need to instruct the lawyer on law or the accountant on taxation. It needs to ensure that the legal and tax inputs address the same family decision and that their implications are understood together.

This distinction protects professional boundaries while reducing fragmentation.

Who Owns the Consolidated View?

The central question is not, "Do we have enough professionals?" It is, "Who owns the consolidated view?"

In some families, the answer may be a financially capable family member. That arrangement can work when the financial structure is relatively simple, the person has sufficient time and the system is documented so that others are not excluded.

In a larger or more complex family, the function may be assigned to an internal finance team, a family-office employee or an external wealth-governance coordinator. The form matters less than the accountability.

The owner of the consolidated view should know what information is current, which decisions are pending, which specialist is responsible, what documents are required and when the family must act. This person or function should not replace professional judgement. It should prevent professional judgement from remaining isolated.

Better Coordination, Not More Noise

The objective is not to invite every professional into every discussion. That would create more administration, not less.

Good coordination is selective. The right professional receives the right information at the right stage. Routine matters are handled through clear responsibilities. Issues that cross boundaries are escalated. The family receives a concise explanation of the decision required rather than a collection of unconnected reports.

This improves the experience for professionals as well. They spend less time requesting basic information, working from inconsistent data or discovering late-stage constraints. Their advice can be more precise because the context is clearer.

The family also gains a more realistic understanding of expertise. No single professional is expected to solve every problem. Specialists are respected for their defined roles, and coordination is treated as a separate responsibility.

The Missing Function

When a family experiences confusion despite having good professionals, the natural response is often to search for a better professional. Sometimes a change is justified. Often, however, the underlying problem will remain because the structure of the relationships has not changed.

The family does not necessarily need another opinion, another report or another institution. It may need an organising function that connects the expertise already present.

More advisors can expand knowledge. Only coordination turns that knowledge into one coherent family decision.

V

Part II — The Shift: From Wealth Management to Wealth Governance

The next stage begins with a change in the question. Instead of starting with a product, the family starts with purpose, ownership, responsibility, documentation and review. This part defines the Family CFO and introduces the Family Wealth Operating System.

VI

CHAPTER 4: From Product Decisions to Governance Decisions

Most financial conversations begin at the point of implementation.

Which account should be opened? Which investment should be selected? Which policy should be purchased? Which property should be sold? Which loan should be repaid first?

These are legitimate questions, but they are rarely the first questions a family should ask. They assume that the purpose, ownership, time horizon, obligations, authority and review process have already been clarified.

In many families, they have not.

A product decision chooses an instrument. A governance decision defines the conditions under which an instrument should be considered, implemented, documented and reviewed.

The difference is important because a technically sound product can still be inappropriate within a poorly defined family decision.

Why Product Questions Feel Easier

Product questions are concrete. They offer a menu, a comparison and the possibility of a quick answer. Governance questions are less comfortable because they require the family to clarify priorities and confront trade-offs.

"Where should we invest?" sounds actionable.

"What is this money required to do, who depends upon it and what other obligations compete for it?" demands a deeper conversation.

A family may want growth, liquidity, tax efficiency, simplicity, protection, control and transferability at the same time. These objectives do not always point in the same direction. The role of governance is not to pretend that every objective can be maximised. It is to make the trade-offs explicit before implementation.

Without that discussion, the product becomes a substitute for the decision.

The family may select something because it is familiar, recently successful, recommended by a trusted contact or readily available through an institution. The decision may later be criticised for performance, when the more fundamental problem was that its intended purpose was never recorded.

The Questions That Come First

Before implementation, a family should be able to answer a small group of governance questions.

What is the purpose? Is the money intended for a known expenditure, long-term wealth building, income, business support, protection, succession or another objective? A broad answer such as "for the future" is rarely sufficient.

Who owns the asset or arrangement? Ownership affects control, reporting, taxation, documentation and succession. The answer should be verified through appropriate records and, where necessary, qualified professionals.

Who depends upon it? An asset may appear to belong to one person while serving several family needs. A decision cannot be understood without identifying the people and obligations connected to it.

When may the money or benefit be required? Time changes the relevance of liquidity, risk and accessibility. The family should distinguish between a distant objective and a commitment that may arise within months.

What risks surround the decision? The family should consider not only market or product risk, but also business exposure, debt, legal uncertainty, concentration, illiquidity, currency, access and dependence upon one decision-maker.

What obligations already exist? A new decision competes with taxes, loan repayments, business commitments, education, family support and planned expenditure. These obligations should be visible before resources are committed.

Who has authority and responsibility? Who approves the decision? Who executes it? Who maintains the records? Who follows up with professionals? Authority without responsibility creates inaction. Responsibility without authority creates frustration.

What must be documented? The family should record the purpose, key assumptions, ownership, professional inputs and review conditions. Documentation should be proportionate, not bureaucratic.

When will the decision be reviewed? A review date or review trigger prevents a temporary decision from becoming permanent through neglect.

These questions do not determine the product. They create the context within which appropriately qualified professionals can assist the family.

Designing a Decision Architecture

A decision architecture is the structure through which important financial choices are made.

At its simplest, it contains five elements: visibility, responsibility, authority, documentation and review.

Visibility means that the family begins with current and relevant facts. Responsibility identifies who must move the matter forward. Authority clarifies who can approve or sign. Documentation records the reasoning and terms. Review determines when the family will examine whether the decision remains appropriate.

Consider a business family evaluating the purchase of another property. A product-led discussion may focus on location, price and financing. A governance-led discussion would also ask whether the property is personal or business-related, which entity or individual should own it, how the purchase affects existing guarantees and liquidity, who will manage it, what records must be maintained and how it fits with succession intentions.

The second discussion does not eliminate the need for property, legal, tax and financing expertise. It ensures that the specialists are solving the same family question.

The architecture can be brief. A one-page decision note may be sufficient for many matters. The discipline lies in requiring the important questions to be answered before execution.

Better Process, Not Guaranteed Outcomes

Governance improves the quality of a decision process. It does not guarantee the result.

Markets change. Businesses underperform. regulations evolve. Family circumstances shift. A carefully governed decision can still produce an unfavourable outcome, just as a poorly governed decision can occasionally succeed.

The value of process is that the family knows why the decision was made, which assumptions were accepted and what would cause it to be reviewed. It can distinguish a bad outcome from a bad process.

This distinction is essential for learning.

When reasoning is undocumented, families judge decisions mainly by recent results. A successful outcome may reinforce careless behaviour. An unsuccessful outcome may cause a sound long-term decision to be abandoned. Governance creates a more disciplined basis for review.

It also reduces retrospective conflict. Family members may still disagree, but the original purpose and authority are visible. The conversation can focus on what has changed rather than on reconstructing what people remember.

Governance Across Family, Business and Jurisdiction

The need for governance increases when financial decisions cross boundaries.

A promoter may use a personally owned asset to support a business borrowing. A family member living abroad may remain connected to assets in India. A parent may fund a child's venture through an arrangement that is neither clearly a gift nor clearly a loan. A property may serve family, business and succession purposes simultaneously.

These decisions cannot be evaluated from one professional perspective alone. They involve ownership, taxation, liquidity, risk, documentation and family expectations.

Governance does not mean that one person provides all answers. It means that the family frames the decision correctly, engages the relevant specialists and records how their inputs fit together.

The family should also recognise that silence is a decision. Allowing an arrangement to continue without review assigns consequences, even if nobody actively chose them.

From Transactions to a System

Many families have good transaction records and weak decision records.

They can produce a statement showing what was purchased, when and at what value. They cannot produce a short explanation of why the decision was made, what need it serves, who relies upon it or when it should be reconsidered.

A transaction record describes movement. A decision record describes intent.

Intent matters because family circumstances evolve. An account opened for a child's education may remain long after the purpose changes. A property acquired for business expansion may later become an investment or succession asset. A reserve established during a period of uncertainty may be absorbed into general funds.

Without a recorded purpose, the family cannot tell whether an arrangement has completed its job.

Governance therefore changes the unit of attention. The family stops viewing each account, asset or product as an isolated item and begins viewing it as part of a continuing decision.

A Better Starting Point

The shift from product decisions to governance decisions is not an argument against financial products. Families need accounts, investments, insurance, credit and legal structures. The point is sequencing.

Implementation should follow purpose. Product selection should follow context. Specialist advice should follow a clearly framed question. Review should follow documentation.

When the order is reversed, the family accumulates arrangements faster than it accumulates understanding.

The more useful question is no longer only, "What should we buy?"

It is, "What system should govern how our family makes, implements and reviews financial decisions?"

VII

CHAPTER 5: What Is a Family CFO?

As family wealth expands, the financial picture often becomes too broad for one specialist and too important to remain coordinated informally.

The family may have professionals for taxation, law, banking, insurance, investments and business finance. Each relationship serves a purpose. Yet someone still has to maintain the consolidated view: what the family owns, what it owes, what risks require attention, which decisions are pending, which documents are missing and which professional must act next.

The Family CFO is the function that owns this view.

It is best understood not as another product provider, but as a financial command-centre, governance and coordination role for the family.

A Descriptive Governance Role

"Family CFO" is a descriptive service and governance model. It is not a statutory or regulatory designation.

The role does not grant authority to perform regulated activities. Investment advice, securities recommendations, legal work, tax advice, accounting, estate documentation, insurance intermediation and other specialised services must be provided by persons holding the qualifications or registrations required for those activities.

The Family CFO's contribution lies elsewhere.

The role consolidates information, helps the family see connections, coordinates specialists, records decisions, tracks actions, establishes review discipline and prepares the system to continue when circumstances change.

In a company, the chief financial officer does not personally audit the accounts, draft every contract, approve every bank facility or make every operating decision. The CFO maintains the integrated financial picture and ensures that specialised work supports the organisation's objectives.

The family version follows a similar logic, while respecting the legal and regulatory boundaries relevant to personal wealth.

What the Family CFO Does

The first responsibility is visibility.

The Family CFO helps create a dependable record of assets, liabilities, ownership, entities, income sources, major obligations, insurance records, documents, professional relationships and pending decisions. This does not mean that every figure is independently verified by the coordinator. It means that the source, date and status of the information are known and specialist verification is obtained where required.

The second responsibility is coordination.

A family matter may require several professionals. The Family CFO helps frame the issue, ensure that the relevant facts are available, identify the professional responsible for each component and bring the implications back into one family-level view. The coordinator does not tell the lawyer how to practise law or the accountant how to interpret tax rules. The coordinator ensures that their work addresses the same underlying decision.

The third responsibility is decision support.

The family must retain authority over its choices. The Family CFO helps clarify the question, document objectives and constraints, compare professional inputs, record the decision and identify the next action. Decision support is not the same as making the decision on behalf of the family.

The fourth responsibility is follow-through.

Many financial weaknesses do not arise from a lack of discussion. They arise because agreed actions remain incomplete. A nomination is to be updated, a document is to be reviewed, a guarantee is to be confirmed, an account is to be reconciled, a professional is to provide an opinion. The Family CFO maintains an action register, assigns owners and brings unresolved matters back for review.

The fifth responsibility is continuity.

The system should not depend entirely upon the founder's memory. The Family CFO helps establish document access, emergency records, contact lists, ownership maps and review routines so that another responsible person can understand the financial structure when required.

What the Family CFO Does Not Do

Clear boundaries protect the family and the professionals involved.

A Family CFO does not automatically replace the family's chartered accountant. The accountant's work may include accounting, taxation, reporting, audit support and entity compliance. The Family CFO uses relevant outputs from that work within the consolidated family picture.

The role does not replace a lawyer. Legal documents, legal opinions, succession structures, ownership disputes and jurisdictional interpretation belong with qualified legal professionals.

It does not replace a banker. Banking operations, lending decisions, custody, account mandates and institutional services remain with the relevant institutions.

It does not replace a mutual fund distributor, SEBI Registered Investment Adviser, insurance professional, portfolio manager or other regulated participant. Each has a defined scope and regulatory context. Where the Family CFO also holds a separate registration or licence, the capacity in which a service is provided should be disclosed clearly and conflicts should be managed transparently.

The Family CFO should not guarantee returns, promise financial outcomes, take undisclosed control of assets or make decisions that belong to the family. Nor should the role become a channel through which every family need is converted into a product sale.

The distinction is simple: the coordinator helps the family govern the decision process. Appropriately authorised professionals perform the regulated or specialised work.

One Point of Coordination

The practical value of the role is often expressed through one point of contact.

This does not mean that every professional reports hierarchically to the Family CFO or that the family stops speaking to specialists. It means that the family has one place where information, decisions and action status are consolidated.

A business owner may not wish to attend separate meetings merely to discover that each professional is waiting for information held by another. The Family CFO can identify what the family needs to decide, gather the relevant inputs and return with a concise decision list.

This saves more than meeting time. It reduces cognitive switching. The family no longer has to remember which part of the story was told to which professional. Important matters are tracked across conversations.

The coordinator also becomes responsible for maintaining the family's "open loops": decisions not yet made, documents not yet completed, confirmations not yet received and changes not yet reflected in the dashboard.

Wealth administration becomes less dependent upon the founder's inbox.

Distinctions from Other Roles

A Family CFO and a family-office administrator can overlap, but they are not identical. Administration focuses heavily on execution, payments, record maintenance and operations. The Family CFO model described here places greater emphasis on governance, coordination, decision visibility and review. In a larger family office, both functions may exist.

A Family CFO and a wealth manager may also overlap in conversation, but the Family CFO is not defined by managing a portfolio. The role covers the connections among business interests, personal assets, liabilities, cash flow, risk, documents, professionals and succession.

A Family CFO and a registered investment adviser are distinct. A registered adviser may provide regulated investment advice within the permitted scope. The Family CFO coordinates the broader family system. A family may engage both, or a properly registered person may perform separate roles with clear disclosures and boundaries.

A Family CFO and a family member serving as financial organiser can perform similar functions. The difference may be capacity, independence, time and continuity. A family member may be entirely suitable where complexity is modest and records are maintained well. External support becomes more valuable when responsibilities are expanding, neutrality is important or the family lacks time.

Discretion, Confidentiality and Trust

The role requires access to sensitive information. The family should therefore examine confidentiality, data security and conflicts with the same care applied to technical competence.

What information will be collected? Where will it be stored? Who can access it? How are permissions withdrawn? What happens when the engagement ends? Which communications are recorded? How are personal and business data separated? How are third-party service providers assessed?

Trust should not rely only on personal comfort. It should be supported by defined processes.

The Family CFO should also be willing to state limits. A coordinator who pretends to be expert in every field creates risk. A credible professional knows when a matter requires legal, tax, regulatory, insurance, cybersecurity or other specialist input.

When the Role May Not Be Necessary

Not every affluent family needs a dedicated Family CFO.

A household with a small number of accounts, clear ownership, limited liabilities, no business complexity, current legal documents and one capable family member maintaining an accessible system may be governed adequately without a separate coordinator.

The need is driven less by net worth than by complexity.

Several entities, cross-border assets, multiple decision-makers, business guarantees, several professionals, incomplete documentation, frequent unresolved actions and dependence upon one person increase the value of a dedicated function.

The family should not adopt the label for prestige. It should adopt the discipline when the cost of coordination has become material.

A Coherent System

The Family CFO is not the most important professional in the family's network. The role is important because it helps the network function as a network.

The accountant should remain excellent at accounting. The lawyer should remain excellent at law. The banker, distributor, registered adviser, insurance professional and business specialist should continue contributing within their defined scopes.

The Family CFO does not replace these specialists. The role helps their specialised work become part of one coherent financial system.

VIII

CHAPTER 6: The Family Wealth Operating System

A list can tell a family what it owns. An operating system tells the family how the parts work together.

This distinction matters because wealth is not static. Income arrives, obligations are paid, assets are acquired, risks change, family members relocate, professionals are appointed and documents become outdated. The family is not managing a photograph. It is managing a moving system.

A Family Wealth Operating System provides the structure through which information enters, decisions are made, responsibilities are assigned, actions are tracked and the financial picture is reviewed.

The model in this book contains six connected engines: Core, Income, Growth, Security, Liquidity and Legacy.

What Makes It an Operating System

An operating system requires more than information.

It needs dependable inputs. The family must know which records are authoritative, when they were updated and where verification is required.

It needs responsibilities. Someone must maintain the asset register, follow up on a legal document, review an insurance record, reconcile a liability and convene the next review.

It needs decision rules. The family should know which matters can be handled routinely, which require joint approval and which require specialist input.

It needs documentation. Important decisions should retain enough context to be understood later.

It needs feedback. Reviews should reveal changes, unresolved actions and emerging risks.

Without these elements, the family may possess an impressive dashboard that gradually becomes another outdated file. The operating system is the process that keeps the information useful.

The Core Engine

The Core Engine establishes the family's financial architecture.

It includes the asset and liability registers, ownership and entity maps, document locations, institutional relationships, professional contacts and decision records. It creates the consolidated family wealth dashboard from which the other engines operate.

The Core Engine is not merely a net-worth statement. A net-worth statement may show values without explaining ownership, accessibility, obligations or document status. The Core Engine provides structure around the numbers.

Its central question is: Can the family reliably see and explain its financial position?

When the answer is unclear, other decisions begin from assumptions. The Growth Engine may consider an investment without understanding concentration. The Liquidity Engine may overestimate accessible resources. The Legacy Engine may rely on ownership information that has not been updated.

Clarity therefore comes before sophistication.

The Income Engine

The Income Engine governs the movement and rhythm of money through the family.

Affluent households may receive salary, business drawings, dividends, rent, professional income and irregular distributions. They may also support parents, children, education, lifestyle commitments, philanthropy and business needs.

The challenge is not always insufficient income. It is the absence of a clear view of what is regular, what is variable, what is committed and what should remain within the business.

The Income Engine records sources, timing, household obligations, major annual commitments and family funding policies. It helps prevent temporary prosperity from creating permanent fixed costs.

Its central question is: Does the family understand how money enters, moves through and leaves the household system?

This engine is distinct from liquidity. Income describes flow. Liquidity describes accessible reserves when timing matters.

The Growth Engine

The Growth Engine governs long-term wealth-building decisions.

It does not begin with a list of products. It begins with purpose, time horizon, obligations, ownership, decision authority and review discipline. It records why an investment-related decision was made, which professional inputs were obtained and what conditions would require reconsideration.

The Growth Engine also addresses behaviour. Families can accumulate unrelated arrangements in response to market narratives, social proof, fear or recent performance. A governed process reduces impulsive decisions without pretending to eliminate uncertainty.

Its central question is: Are long-term decisions being made and reviewed within a consistent family framework?

Product selection and regulated advice remain with appropriately authorised professionals. The engine ensures that implementation is connected to the family's wider position.

The Security Engine

The Security Engine identifies risks that may disrupt the family or business.

These risks include death, disability, illness, loss of income, personal guarantees, debt obligations, key-person dependency, business continuity, cyber threats, fraud, property exposures and the concentration of knowledge in one individual.

The engine creates a risk register and maps existing protection, responsibilities, documentation and claim readiness. Insurance may form part of the response, but the engine is broader than insurance.

Its central question is: Which foreseeable events could destabilise the family, and who is responsible for preparing the response?

Security does not mean eliminating all risk. That is impossible. It means recognising material exposures before they become emergencies and coordinating the appropriate professionals.

The Liquidity Engine

The Liquidity Engine protects access to resources.

A family can have a high net worth and still face financial stress if most assets are illiquid, pledged, business-dependent, legally restricted or difficult to access at short notice.

The engine distinguishes emergency liquidity, opportunity liquidity and reserves for planned expenditure. It considers timing, certainty, accessibility, currency and replenishment.

Its central question is: Can the family access appropriate resources when circumstances require action?

The word "appropriate" matters. Every available balance is not necessarily free capital. Some resources support business operations, taxes or near-term commitments. The engine prevents the family from confusing visible money with deployable money.

The Legacy Engine

The Legacy Engine prepares wealth, knowledge and responsibility to continue beyond the first generation.

It includes wills and estate documents, ownership and nomination records, executors, business succession, digital assets, family communication, emergency records and coordination with legal and tax professionals.

The engine is not limited to what happens after death. It also addresses incapacity, withdrawal from active decision-making and the gradual transfer of financial responsibility.

Its central question is: Can the family's financial system continue when the current decision-maker no longer performs the role?

A successful transfer gives the next generation more than assets. It provides context, access, responsibility and a process for making decisions.

How the Engines Interact

The engines are separate for clarity, not because family life is separate.

A business owner considers purchasing a second home abroad. The Core Engine records ownership and documents. The Income Engine assesses recurring costs. The Growth Engine examines how the decision fits with long-term priorities. The Security Engine considers liabilities and risk. The Liquidity Engine reviews the timing of payments and accessible reserves. The Legacy Engine considers future ownership and jurisdictional implications.

One decision touches every engine.

This is why a family can create imbalance by strengthening one area while ignoring another. It may pursue growth while allowing ownership records to become unclear. It may maintain substantial liquidity while neglecting succession. It may purchase protection without maintaining claim-ready documentation. It may create detailed dashboards without a review rhythm.

The operating system prevents the family from treating interconnected matters as isolated transactions.

Sequencing the Work

Implementation should normally begin with visibility.

The family identifies members, entities, assets, liabilities, documents, professionals and immediate deadlines. It then examines urgent risks, access concerns and liquidity vulnerabilities. Income and long-term decision processes are organised. Legacy and continuity work develops as ownership and responsibilities become clearer.

This sequence is not rigid.

A severe protection gap, legal deadline, liquidity shortage or succession event may require immediate specialist attention before the full dashboard is completed. Governance should improve priorities, not delay urgent action.

The family should distinguish between two tracks: building the system and resolving urgent issues. Both can proceed at the same time, provided ownership is clear.

An Event Across Six Engines

Consider an illustrative family in which the founder plans to step back from an operating business while one child moves overseas and another assumes a management role.

The apparent issue is succession. In practice, the transition affects the entire operating system.

The Core Engine must update entity roles, authorised signatories, ownership records and professional contacts. The Income Engine must distinguish the founder's future household funding from business cash flow. The Growth Engine must record how family capital will be governed after the founder reduces involvement. The Security Engine must review key-person dependency, guarantees and operational authority. The Liquidity Engine must ensure that personal commitments do not depend entirely upon uncertain business distributions. The Legacy Engine must align legal documents, communication and future responsibility.

No single specialist owns the entire transition. The operating system ensures that the family sees it as one connected event.

Infrastructure, Not a Collection of Services

The Six Engines are not a menu from which a family purchases whichever item appears attractive. They are a way of organising attention.

Some engines will require more work than others. A young entrepreneurial family may focus heavily on income, security and liquidity. A mature business family may require deeper ownership, governance and succession work. A Global Indian family may face cross-border complexity across every engine.

The purpose is not uniformity. It is completeness.

The Six Engines form the infrastructure through which family wealth can be understood, governed and carried forward.

IX

Part III — The Six TFS Engines

The six engines organise family wealth into distinct but connected areas of governance. Each engine has a specific job. Together, they create the infrastructure through which information, decisions, risks, liquidity and continuity can be managed as one system.

X

CHAPTER 7: The Core Engine: Clarity Before Strategy

Every financial strategy rests upon a set of facts.

What does the family own? What does it owe? In whose name is each asset held? Which entities are involved? Where are the records? Who can operate the accounts? Which figures are current and which are estimates?

When the facts are incomplete, strategy begins with assumptions. The Core Engine exists to replace those assumptions with a dependable financial architecture.

From Documents to Visibility

Affluent families usually possess substantial documentation. The problem is not always absence. It is usability.

A title deed in a bank locker is useful only if the family knows that it exists, what property it relates to, whether any loan closure records should accompany it and who is authorised to access it. An account statement is useful only if the account is connected to an owner, purpose, institution and review date. A legal document is useful only if the family knows whether it reflects current circumstances.

The Core Engine therefore does not begin by collecting paper for its own sake. It begins by designing a map.

The map identifies each material asset, liability, entity, relationship and document. It records the source and date of information. It distinguishes confirmed facts from items awaiting verification.

This distinction is valuable. Families often mix certainty and assumption in the same spreadsheet. An ownership percentage copied from memory may appear beside a bank balance downloaded that morning, with no indication that the two figures have different levels of reliability.

A governed record makes status visible.

The Family Asset Register

The asset register is the foundation of the Core Engine.

For each material asset, it may record the asset category, description, owner, co-owner, entity, institution, location, identification reference, acquisition date, approximate value, income produced, encumbrance, document location, information source, last update and responsible person.

The purpose is not to create a valuation report. Values may be estimated and should be labelled accordingly. The purpose is to ensure that the family can identify what exists and connect it to ownership, obligations and records.

An asset register should include more than financial accounts. Depending upon the family, it may cover business interests, real estate, loans given, valuable movable property, intellectual property, overseas assets and other material rights.

The register should also explain exclusions. If the family decides not to include personal-use items below a defined threshold, that decision should be stated. A clear scope is better than an apparently complete list built from inconsistent assumptions.

Liabilities, Guarantees and Obligations

Families tend to remember assets more readily than obligations.

The liability register should include loans, overdrafts, property finance, business borrowings with personal exposure, guarantees, tax dues under discussion, contractual commitments and material amounts owed to or by related parties.

Not every obligation is a recorded loan. A promoter's personal guarantee may create exposure without an immediate cash outflow. A commitment to fund a child's education or support a family member may not appear on a balance sheet but may affect liquidity and decision-making.

The Core Engine does not decide how every obligation should be treated. It makes the obligation visible and identifies the professional input required.

Liabilities should be connected to purpose, borrower, lender, security, guarantor, repayment schedule, document location and review status. A single total is insufficient if the family cannot explain what created it.

Ownership and Entity Maps

Ownership is the bridge between financial information and legal reality.

A family may speak of "our property" or "our business," while the records show a more specific arrangement. An asset may be held individually, jointly, through a company, partnership, LLP, trust or another structure. Control, economic benefit, legal title and family expectation may not always align.

The Core Engine records the available facts without offering legal conclusions. Where ownership, beneficial interest, nomination, succession or control is uncertain, the matter should be referred to an appropriately qualified legal or tax professional.

An entity map is especially useful for business families. It shows which family members own or control each entity, how the entities relate, which assets and liabilities sit within them and which professionals maintain their records.

The map often reveals complexity that no single entity's accounts can show.

It may also reveal dependence. Several entities may require the signature of one person. A family member may hold a role for historical reasons but have little current involvement. An operating business may use an asset owned elsewhere without the arrangement being documented clearly.

Visibility does not resolve these matters. It makes resolution possible.

The Family Wealth Dashboard

The dashboard converts registers into a decision view.

It should not reproduce every detail. Its purpose is to show the current position, material changes, unresolved risks, upcoming obligations, pending decisions and responsible persons.

A useful dashboard may include:

- Consolidated asset and liability summaries.
- Ownership and entity highlights.
- Liquidity available for defined purposes.
- Major income sources and annual commitments.
- Material insurance and risk records.
- Document and succession status.

- Upcoming renewals and deadlines.
- Open actions, owners and target dates.
- The date of the next review.

The dashboard should distinguish information from interpretation. A balance is a fact at a stated date. Whether the balance is adequate for a family purpose is a judgement that may require further analysis or professional input.

A dashboard that attempts to answer every question becomes unreadable. The detailed registers should remain available beneath it.

The family should be able to move from summary to source.

Decision Logs and Open Actions

Financial history is often preserved through transaction records but not through reasoning.

A decision log records the date, question, objective, information considered, professionals consulted, decision-maker, conclusion, assumptions, implementation owner and review trigger.

This need not be lengthy. The purpose is to preserve context.

An action register performs a different function. It records what must be done, who owns the action, which professional is involved, the target date, current status and any dependency.

The distinction prevents a common failure: a decision is made, everyone leaves the meeting satisfied and nobody completes the next step.

Open actions should remain visible until they are completed, cancelled or replaced by a new decision. They should not disappear merely because a review period has ended.

Data Ownership and Access

The Core Engine contains sensitive information. Its design must therefore include security, not add security later.

The family should decide where the records are stored, who can view them, who can edit them, how changes are logged, how backups are maintained and how access is revoked. Personal and business information may require separate permissions.

Convenience should not lead to casual sharing of passwords or confidential documents. A password manager, encrypted storage, secure institutional access and professional cybersecurity guidance may be appropriate, depending upon the family's circumstances.

The family should also decide what a trusted person needs during an emergency. Full access may not be necessary. A secure index showing where information is held and whom to contact may be sufficient for certain records.

Data ownership should be clear when an external coordinator is involved. The family should retain control over its information and be able to obtain a usable copy when the engagement ends.

The Risk of an Outdated Dashboard

The first version of a dashboard often creates enthusiasm. The family sees its financial life in one place and assumes the problem has been solved.

Then the system ages.

A new account is opened but not added. A loan is repaid but not marked closed. A family member relocates. An insurance policy changes. A property is sold. A professional relationship ends. The dashboard remains visually impressive and factually obsolete.

An outdated dashboard can be more dangerous than no dashboard because it carries the appearance of authority.

The Core Engine therefore requires a maintenance rhythm. Administrative changes may be recorded monthly or as they occur. Material changes should trigger updates. A quarterly review can reconcile the summary, while an annual review examines the underlying structure in greater depth.

Each field should have an owner. "The family" is not an owner. A named person or role must be responsible.

When Ownership Matters More Than Value

Consider an illustrative family that owned two valuable commercial properties. Both appeared on the family's net-worth statement at reasonable estimates.

During a review, the family discovered that the first property was owned jointly by the parents, while the second was held by an entity in which the next generation had different economic interests. One property supported a business borrowing. The other generated rent used for household expenses. The family had treated the properties as interchangeable because their values were similar.

They were not interchangeable.

Their ownership, obligations, income purpose and succession implications differed. A valuation-only view had concealed the distinction.

The Core Engine did not decide what the family should do with the properties. It made the facts visible so that legal, tax, lending and family discussions could begin from the same picture.

Clarity Before Strategy

A family does not need perfect data before making any decision. Urgent matters will sometimes require action while records are still being assembled.

But uncertainty should be labelled, not ignored.

The Core Engine gives the family a disciplined starting point. It reveals what is known, what is missing, who must verify it and how the information connects.

A family cannot govern what it cannot reliably see, identify and explain.

XI

CHAPTER 8: The Income Engine: Cash Flow, Lifestyle and Family Funding

A family can have a high income and still have little understanding of how money moves through its life.

This is particularly common in entrepreneurial households. Personal income may not arrive as a fixed monthly amount. Money may flow through salary, drawings, dividends, rent, reimbursements, partnership distributions or irregular transfers. Family expenditure may be met partly from personal accounts and partly through business arrangements. Large annual commitments may be known individually but never viewed together.

The Income Engine brings order to this movement.

Its purpose is not to impose a restrictive household budget on an affluent family. It is to make the rhythm of income, expenditure and family funding visible enough to support deliberate decisions.

Income, Cash Flow and Wealth Are Different

Income is what the family earns or receives.

Cash flow describes when money actually enters and leaves accounts.

Wealth is the stock of assets and economic interests the family has accumulated.

A family may be wealthy but experience uneven cash flow. It may report substantial income while most of the money remains within a business. It may have a valuable property portfolio but rely on irregular rent receipts. It may receive a large annual distribution and spend as though the amount arrives every month.

These distinctions matter because household commitments are usually continuous even when income is not.

School fees, staff salaries, loan instalments, maintenance, family support, travel, health costs and lifestyle expenses follow their own calendars. The family needs a system that connects irregular inflows to regular obligations.

Without that system, the household may repeatedly draw upon whichever account has money at the moment. The family remains solvent, but its decisions become reactive.

Mapping the Sources

The Income Engine begins with a map of sources.

For each material source, the family may record who receives it, whether it is regular or variable, the expected timing, the account into which it arrives, the degree of certainty and any conditions attached to it.

A salary is different from a discretionary business distribution. Rent is different from a one-time asset sale. A dividend from a family company is different from reimbursement of expenses. Loan proceeds are not income merely because they increase an account balance.

This classification prevents a common error: treating every inflow as available household income.

Business families should also distinguish between money the family can legally and prudently withdraw and money the business requires for working capital, tax, debt service, growth or contingencies. The business may appear cash-rich on one date while having substantial obligations shortly afterwards.

The Income Engine does not make tax or company-law determinations. Those matters require professional guidance. It ensures that the household does not confuse access with entitlement or temporary balances with sustainable income.

The Annual Commitment View

Monthly expense tracking is useful for some families, but it is often insufficient for affluent households.

The more revealing document is an annual commitment calendar.

This calendar includes recurring monthly expenditure and larger periodic obligations: school or university fees, insurance premiums, property taxes, club subscriptions, planned travel, vehicle replacement, medical costs, support to parents, family celebrations, philanthropy and business-related commitments that are funded personally.

The family should distinguish between:

- Essential commitments.
- Contractual obligations.
- Lifestyle expenditure.
- Family support.
- Planned discretionary spending.
- Exceptional or non-recurring expenditure.

The distinction is not intended to judge spending. It helps the family understand which commitments can be adjusted and which cannot.

A high annual income may appear ample until irregular obligations are placed on one timeline. Conversely, a family may discover that its cash flow is more resilient than it assumed because certain large expenses are optional or already funded separately.

Visibility replaces vague comfort or vague anxiety with a usable picture.

When Business and Family Cash Become Entangled

The line between business and household finances often becomes blurred during the early years of an enterprise.

The founder funds the business personally. The business pays expenses on behalf of the family. The family withdraws money when required. Informal balances accumulate between promoters and entities. These arrangements may be understandable when the business is small and one person controls both sides.

As the business and family grow, the same informality becomes difficult to govern.

The household may become dependent upon irregular withdrawals. The business may support a lifestyle that is not reflected in a clear compensation or distribution policy. Family members may form different expectations about access to business resources. The accountant may be able to record the transactions, but the family still lacks a policy.

The Income Engine encourages a clear conversation:

What regular amount is intended to support the household? Which business payments are legitimate business expenses? How are exceptional family needs approved? What distributions are discretionary? What happens during a weak business year? Which personal commitments should not depend upon business cash flow?

The answers will differ by family and must be consistent with legal and tax requirements. The governance principle is universal: recurring household life should not depend upon unexplained transfers.

Family Funding Policies

Affluent families often support more people than the immediate household.

Parents may receive regular assistance. Adult children may receive education funding, housing support or capital for a venture. Extended family members may seek help during emergencies. Philanthropic commitments may be meaningful and recurring.

Generosity becomes difficult when expectations are not defined.

A family funding policy does not need to be a legal document. It can be a clear internal understanding covering who may request support, which types of support are normally considered, who approves material amounts, whether money is intended as a gift or loan, what documentation is appropriate and when the arrangement will be reviewed.

The policy protects relationships by reducing ambiguity.

Without clarity, one family member may view an amount as temporary while another views it as permanent. A founder may make commitments that the spouse or next generation does not understand. Support given through a business may create accounting or governance questions. The family may say yes repeatedly because no one has defined a decision process.

The purpose is not to make generosity mechanical. It is to ensure that generosity remains sustainable and understood.

Lifestyle Inflation and Fixed Commitments

Success naturally changes lifestyle.

The risk arises when temporary income creates permanent fixed costs.

A strong business year may lead to a larger home, additional staff, new memberships, higher education commitments or recurring travel expectations. These choices may be entirely affordable while performance remains strong. They become difficult when income is cyclical or concentrated in one source.

The Income Engine does not prescribe how a family should live. It asks whether the household's fixed commitments are aligned with the durability of its income.

A useful review separates core lifestyle costs from variable expenditure and identifies which commitments would continue during a weak year. The family can then decide whether income sources, reserves and protection arrangements support that level of obligation.

This conversation is especially important for first-generation wealth creators. Their personal lifestyle may evolve faster than the business's ability to provide stable distributions independent of the founder.

Shared Understanding Between Spouses

In many families, one spouse manages income and the other manages expenditure. Both may be capable, but neither sees the entire flow.

A governed system does not require both spouses to approve every payment. It requires both to understand the broad structure: main income sources, fixed commitments, major upcoming expenses, access arrangements and the person responsible for administration.

This shared understanding reduces dependence and improves continuity.

It also changes the quality of discussion. Instead of debating isolated expenses, the family can discuss how spending, business distributions, liquidity and long-term priorities fit together.

Where adult children receive material support, the family may also decide what they should understand. Transparency need not mean unrestricted access. It means that expectations and responsibilities are deliberate.

An Uneven Income Year

Consider an illustrative family whose income came primarily from a trading business.

The family's lifestyle had been funded through a combination of salary, reimbursements and irregular promoter withdrawals. During strong quarters, large amounts were transferred to personal accounts. During weak quarters, household payments were met from accumulated balances.

The system worked until the business faced a year in which inventory requirements increased and customer payments slowed. The family remained wealthy, but household cash flow became unpredictable.

A review showed that the problem was not simply lower income. The family had no agreed household funding amount, no annual commitment calendar and no rule separating business reserves from personal access. Several large expenses were due in the same quarter.

The solution began with governance. The family and its professionals clarified regular compensation, mapped annual household obligations, identified exceptional expenses and established a process for discretionary distributions. The business and family could then plan separately without pretending they were unrelated.

The family did not need to reduce every expense. It needed to understand which expenses depended upon which income.

Dependable Income Is Governed Income

The Income Engine is not a judgement on lifestyle and not a demand for minute-by-minute expense tracking.

It is a system for making the family's financial rhythm visible.

When sources, timing, obligations and funding rules are understood, the family can make decisions without repeatedly asking whether a temporary account balance represents permanent capacity.

Income becomes dependable only when the family understands its rhythm, obligations and decision rules.

XII

CHAPTER 9: The Growth Engine: Building Wealth with Discipline

Growth is the part of finance that attracts the most attention.

Markets move daily. New opportunities are presented constantly. Performance can be measured, compared and discussed. Families naturally want their capital to grow.

Yet long-term wealth is not built by product selection alone. It is also shaped by the discipline surrounding purpose, behaviour, decision-making and review.

The Growth Engine governs that discipline.

It does not provide a portfolio, security recommendation or return target. It creates the framework within which appropriately authorised professionals can help the family make and implement investment-related decisions.

Growth Is Not a Competition for the Highest Return

A return cannot be evaluated in isolation from the purpose of the money.

An arrangement intended to meet a near-term obligation has a different job from capital intended for a distant objective. Money supporting household income has a different role from capital the family can leave untouched through uncertainty. A business owner with substantial exposure to one industry may need to consider that exposure when evaluating the rest of the family's financial position.

The Growth Engine therefore begins by asking what the capital is meant to do.

The answer should be more specific than "create wealth." It may relate to long-term family independence, retirement, education, future business capital, intergenerational transfer, philanthropy or another objective.

Purpose provides a basis for professional analysis. Without it, the family is tempted to compare every holding against whichever asset has performed best recently.

This can turn investment review into a permanent search for regret.

The Investment Decision Record

A useful governance tool is the investment decision record.
For a material decision, the record may include:

- The purpose of the money.
- The intended time horizon.
- Ownership.
- Expected liquidity needs.
- Relevant family or business obligations.
- Key risks discussed.
- Professional inputs obtained.
- Fees, taxation, liquidity and complexity considerations.
- The person who approved the decision.
- The implementation responsibility.

- The review date or trigger.

The record does not need to predict the future. It preserves the logic that existed when the decision was made.

This is especially valuable during periods of market stress. The family can return to the original purpose and assumptions rather than reacting only to recent movement.

It is equally valuable after strong performance. Success can create overconfidence. A documented process reminds the family that a favourable outcome does not validate every risk or assumption.

Accumulation Without Architecture

Many affluent families do not have one investment portfolio. They have several collections.

One collection was created by a banker. Another developed through a distributor. A third contains legacy holdings. A fourth sits in a company. Overseas assets may be maintained separately. Real estate and business interests may dominate the family's actual economic exposure but remain outside the investment conversation.

Each collection may be reasonable. The family's weakness lies in the absence of an architecture connecting them.

The Growth Engine does not assume that every asset should be consolidated at one institution. Institutional diversification, access, family preference and specialist capability may justify multiple relationships. What should be consolidated is the view.

The family should know why each relationship exists, what role each pool of capital serves, who owns it, how it is reviewed and how it fits with the family's wider exposures.

Without that view, the same risk can be repeated through different channels while appearing diversified on separate statements.

Behaviour Is Part of Governance

Financial knowledge does not eliminate emotional decision-making.

Successful entrepreneurs may be particularly vulnerable to certain patterns. Confidence built through business success can be carried into unfamiliar financial areas. A founder accustomed to acting quickly may become impatient with long-term processes. A family may follow opportunities introduced through trusted social relationships without applying the same discipline used in the operating business.

Fear creates the opposite reaction. During uncertainty, the family may delay every decision or abandon a long-term plan because recent results feel uncomfortable.

The Growth Engine creates behavioural guardrails.

These may include requiring a written purpose, defining who can approve a material commitment, obtaining specialist input, allowing a cooling-off period for unfamiliar opportunities, recording what would cause the decision to be reconsidered and reviewing concentration across the whole family.

Guardrails do not remove emotion. They prevent emotion from becoming the only decision process.

Reviewing More Than Performance

Performance matters, but it is not the only review question.

A governed review may also ask:

Does the holding still serve its intended purpose? Has the family's time horizon changed? Has ownership changed? Is the liquidity appropriate for the objective? Have fees, taxation, regulation or complexity changed? Has the family's business exposure increased? Is the decision still understood by the people responsible for it? Is the information current? Does the arrangement create an administrative or succession burden that was not anticipated?

These questions help distinguish a temporary performance disappointment from a structural problem.

They also help identify holdings that have become "financial furniture"—arrangements that remain in place because they are familiar, not because the family has made a current decision to retain them.

Any recommendation to continue, change or exit an investment-related arrangement should be made within the appropriate regulatory and professional framework. The Growth Engine ensures that the question is framed and documented properly.

Concentration Awareness

Family wealth is often concentrated by design.

A founder may have most of the family's economic value in the business. A property family may hold substantial real-estate exposure. A senior executive may have compensation linked to one employer. A Global Indian family may have assets and liabilities concentrated in particular currencies or jurisdictions.

Concentration is not automatically an error. It may be the source of wealth creation.

The governance requirement is awareness.

The family should understand where economic outcomes depend upon the same underlying factor. Two assets can have different names and still share the same risk. A business, property and personal guarantee may all depend upon one local market. Several financial holdings may respond similarly to one economic event.

The Growth Engine records these connections so that appropriately qualified professionals can consider them. It does not prescribe a percentage or claim that all concentration should be eliminated.

Coordinating the Professionals

Investment-related decisions may involve a mutual fund distributor, SEBI Registered Investment Advisor, portfolio manager, banker, tax professional, lawyer, accountant or overseas specialist.

The Family CFO framework should clarify the role in which each person is acting.

Who is providing regulated advice? Who is distributing a product? Who is executing? Who is providing tax or legal input? How is each professional compensated? Which conflicts should be disclosed? Who maintains the family-level record?

Clear roles protect the family from assuming that one person has considered matters outside that person's scope.

The family should also resist the temptation to ask every professional the same broad question and then choose the most attractive answer. A better process frames specific questions, provides consistent information and reconciles the implications.

An Unconnected Collection

Consider an illustrative senior professional who had accumulated investments through employers, banks, distributors and personal decisions over twenty years.

The holdings were spread across several institutions. Some were intended for retirement, some for children and some had no recorded purpose. A large portion of the family's wealth was also linked to the executive's employer through compensation and career income.

The problem was not that the family had chosen obviously unsuitable products. The problem was that no one could explain the portfolio as a whole.

During the governance review, the family first classified holdings by ownership, purpose, liquidity, decision-maker and professional relationship. The exercise revealed duplication, concentration and accounts that had not been reviewed for years. These findings were then referred to appropriately authorised professionals for specific advice.

The value of the Growth Engine appeared before any implementation decision. The family moved from a collection of statements to a coherent set of questions.

Discipline Creates Continuity

Long-term wealth building will always involve uncertainty. Governance cannot forecast markets or guarantee outcomes.

It can, however, ensure that the family knows why decisions are made, who is responsible, how specialist input is used and what conditions require review.

Sustainable growth depends not only upon what a family owns, but upon the discipline governing why it owns it and how the decision is reviewed.

XIII

CHAPTER 10: The Security Engine: Risk Before Return

Families naturally prefer to discuss what may go right.

Growth, expansion, income and opportunity are energising. Risk discussions can feel negative, especially when the family is healthy, the business is performing and obligations are being met.

The Security Engine does not begin from pessimism. It begins from responsibility.

Its purpose is to identify events that could destabilise the family or business, understand the existing response and ensure that material gaps are addressed through the appropriate professionals before the event occurs.

Risk Awareness Without Fear

A risk register is not a list of disasters.

It is a structured record of exposures, their potential effect, the existing response, the person responsible and the next review.

The family may consider risks involving:

- Death or disability.
- Serious illness.
- Loss of income.
- Business interruption.
- Key-person dependency.
- Personal guarantees.
- Debt and contingent liabilities.
- Property and liability exposure.
- Cyberattack and fraud.
- Access to accounts and documents.
- Dependence upon one person's knowledge.
- Legal or regulatory change.
- Cross-border disruption.

The purpose is not to calculate every possible loss. It is to identify which events deserve preparation because their consequences could be material.

Risk should be discussed in proportion. A rare event with limited effect may require little action. A familiar event with severe consequences may require immediate attention. The family should also distinguish between risks it can absorb, risks it can reduce, risks it can transfer and risks it must monitor.

These decisions require judgement and, in many cases, specialist input.

Personal and Business Risk Are Connected

For entrepreneurs, the line between personal and business risk is often thin.

A founder may have given personal guarantees for company borrowing. A personally owned property may support a business facility. Household income may depend upon one operating company. The business may depend heavily upon the founder's relationships or technical knowledge. A family member may hold formal responsibility in an entity without understanding the role.

A business problem can therefore become a family problem quickly.

The Security Engine maps these connections.

It records which liabilities have personal exposure, which assets are pledged, which individuals are essential to operations, what authority exists during incapacity and how the family's household obligations would be met if business distributions stopped.

This is not a substitute for legal, lending, insurance or business-continuity advice. It ensures that the family recognises the questions.

A personal risk review that ignores the business is incomplete for a promoter family.

Insurance as Part of a Wider Risk System

Insurance may transfer certain financial risks, but the existence of policies does not prove that the family is protected.

A governed review begins with the exposure, not the product.

What event is the policy intended to address? Who owns the policy? Who is insured? Who is the nominee or beneficiary? What are the terms, exclusions and disclosure requirements? Are premiums current? Where are the records? Does a responsible family member know how to initiate a claim? Has the family's position changed since the policy was obtained?

The answers should be confirmed through the policy documents and appropriately licensed professionals.

The review should also distinguish between adequacy and claim readiness.

A family may possess substantial coverage but be unable to locate documents or explain the claim process. Medical, financial or business disclosures may require careful verification. Policies may be owned by individuals or entities with different implications. Nominations may be outdated.

The Security Engine records these matters and tracks specialist follow-through. It does not recommend a particular insurer, policy or sum assured.

Liabilities and Guarantees

Debt is visible when an instalment is paid each month. Guarantees are less visible because they may remain dormant.

A promoter may sign a guarantee during a business expansion and treat it as a formality. Years later, the facility may change, but the family's risk records may not. A property may remain linked to an obligation even after the family believes the matter is closed. A co-borrower or guarantor may not understand the extent of responsibility.

The Security Engine maintains a liability and guarantee schedule connected to the Core Engine.

For each material exposure, the family should know the borrower, lender, purpose, security, guarantor, outstanding status, key terms, document location and person responsible for review.

Questions regarding enforceability, release, documentation and legal consequence belong with qualified professionals. The governance failure is allowing the exposure to remain invisible.

Key-Person and Knowledge Risk

Some families insure physical assets carefully and leave the most valuable operating dependency unaddressed.

The founder may be the only person who can approve payments, negotiate with lenders, understand family obligations, access institutional relationships and explain the business.

This creates key-person risk in both commercial and family administration.

Preparation may include delegated authority, documented processes, second-line leadership, emergency contacts, access protocols, professional coordination and, where appropriate, insurance reviewed through licensed professionals.

The objective is not to remove the founder from decision-making. It is to prevent the family and business from becoming unable to operate during temporary or permanent absence.

Knowledge risk also exists outside the founder. A long-serving employee may control payroll. A family member may alone understand overseas accounts. An assistant may hold the only organised document index.

The Security Engine asks a practical question: if this person were unavailable tomorrow, which essential functions would stop?

Cybersecurity, Fraud and Access

Modern family wealth is partly digital.

Banking, investments, tax records, company filings, insurance documents and professional communication may be accessed through devices and online platforms. Convenience creates new forms of exposure.

The family should consider device security, password practices, multi-factor authentication, phishing, social engineering, email compromise, unauthorised sharing and the security of external service providers.

Cybersecurity should not be reduced to a list of passwords stored in a spreadsheet. The family may require a reputable password manager, secure recovery procedures, role-based access, encrypted backups and professional guidance.

Access during an emergency must also be designed carefully. Giving several people unrestricted access can create as much risk as giving nobody access. The family should decide what information a trusted person needs, how authority will be verified and which institutional procedures apply.

The Security Engine records the system and the responsible persons. It does not bypass legal or institutional controls.

A Risk Map in Practice

Consider an illustrative family whose wealth depended heavily upon a logistics business.

The founder managed lender relationships, approved major payments and held most property records. The company had insurance policies, the family had personal policies and the business maintained several credit facilities. On paper, the family appeared well protected.

A risk-map exercise revealed connections that separate reviews had missed.

The founder had given personal guarantees. One commercial property used by the business was owned jointly with the spouse. Household cash flow depended upon discretionary business transfers. The operations head understood the business but had no authority over key banking matters. Policy information existed, but the family had no consolidated record of ownership, exclusions, nominees or claim contacts. Important digital access depended upon the founder's phone.

The exercise did not produce one product recommendation. It produced a sequence of professional questions and governance actions: verify guarantee status, review authority, document access, map policy records, clarify household funding and create an emergency contact process.

The family's risk did not disappear. Its preparedness improved.

Security Protects the System

Risk planning should not become a fear-driven search for absolute certainty. No family can insure, document or diversify away every possible event.

The objective is resilience.

The Security Engine helps the family distinguish material exposures from background uncertainty, assign responsibility and coordinate the appropriate response.

Its purpose is not to eliminate uncertainty, but to prevent foreseeable risks from destabilising everything the family has built.

XIV

CHAPTER 11: The Liquidity Engine: Survival, Opportunity and Flexibility

Net worth and liquidity are often spoken of as though they were interchangeable.

They are not.

A family may own valuable businesses, properties and long-term assets while having limited access to money at the moment it is required. Assets may be illiquid, pledged, jointly owned, held through entities, located in another jurisdiction or intended for a purpose that makes immediate use inappropriate.

The Liquidity Engine prepares the family for timing.

Its central concern is not how much the family owns, but what resources can be accessed, with what certainty, within which period and without creating unnecessary damage elsewhere.

The Difference Between Wealth and Access

A high-value asset can be economically important and operationally unavailable.

A property may take months to sell. A business interest may be valuable but unsuitable for partial liquidation. A financial asset may be subject to process, taxation, market conditions or an intended long-term purpose. An overseas account may involve access, currency or reporting considerations. A large company balance may be required for working capital and may not be available to the household.

Liquidity therefore has four dimensions:

- Amount.
- Accessibility.
- Timing.
- Certainty.

A family that looks only at amount can overestimate its capacity.

The Liquidity Engine labels resources by purpose and access rather than treating every balance as one pool.

Three Forms of Liquidity

The first form is emergency liquidity.

This supports the family through events such as illness, temporary loss of income, urgent travel, household disruption or an unexpected requirement. Its value lies in speed and reliability.

The second form is opportunity liquidity.

This is capital the family has deliberately kept available to consider a business, property or other opportunity without disrupting essential obligations. Opportunity liquidity is not an excuse to keep every resource idle. It is a governance choice to preserve the ability to act.

The third form is planned-expenditure liquidity.

This supports known commitments such as education, taxes, property payments, large family events, capital expenditure or retirement-related transitions. The expenditure may not be urgent, but the timing is sufficiently clear that the family should not depend upon a last-minute decision.

These categories can overlap, but naming them prevents one reserve from being promised to several purposes simultaneously.

Liquidity Floors

A liquidity floor is the minimum level of accessible resources the family intends to maintain for a defined purpose.

The level cannot be prescribed generically. It depends upon income stability, business exposure, household commitments, health considerations, debt, insurance, family support, jurisdiction and the availability of credit or other resources.

The governance process is more important than a universal formula.

What obligations must continue if income is interrupted? Which expenses are unavoidable? How quickly can other resources be accessed? Which funds are legally or practically restricted? What business needs must not be confused with household liquidity? Who may authorise use of the reserve? How will it be replenished?

A liquidity floor should have an owner and a review trigger. If the reserve is used, the family should know whether replenishment is automatic, gradual or subject to a new decision.

Without a rule, temporary use can become permanent depletion.

Stress-Testing the Family's Access

Liquidity stress-testing asks what would happen under a small number of plausible scenarios.

What if business distributions stop for six months? What if a major medical payment is required before reimbursement? What if a property transaction is delayed? What if an overseas family member needs support? What if a tax or legal obligation arises at the same time as a planned expenditure?

The purpose is not to forecast every emergency. It is to test whether the family's access assumptions are realistic.

A stress test should examine the sequence of resources, not merely the total amount. Which account would be used first? Who can operate it? Are there institutional limits? Does use of one resource create a tax, legal, market or business consequence that requires professional review? What documentation would be required?

The exercise often reveals that a resource described as "available" is available only under ideal conditions.

Personal and Business Liquidity

Business owners frequently treat the company as the ultimate reserve.

This may work during stable periods. It becomes dangerous when the household and business need cash at the same time.

A downturn may reduce business collections while increasing working-capital requirements. The founder may then discover that the resource expected to support the family is required to protect the enterprise. Personal guarantees or lender restrictions may further reduce flexibility.

The Liquidity Engine separates the two views.

The business requires its own treasury and contingency process. The household requires its own accessible resources and funding policy. The two systems can support each other deliberately, but they should not be treated as one undifferentiated balance.

This separation also improves family communication. The spouse and next generation can understand that a successful business is not the same as an immediately available household reserve.

Planned Expenditure and Forced Decisions

Many liquidity problems are not caused by unexpected events. They are caused by expected events funded too late.

Education payments, taxes, property instalments, business capital, large ceremonies and retirement transitions are often known well in advance. Yet the family may postpone funding decisions because overall wealth appears sufficient.

When the date arrives, the family uses the most convenient source. It may borrow unnecessarily, sell under pressure, interrupt a long-term arrangement or draw money from a business at an inconvenient time.

The governance failure occurred months earlier, when the family did not connect the expenditure date to an accessible reserve.

Planned-expenditure liquidity protects the family from converting a known commitment into an artificial emergency.

Currency and Jurisdiction

Global families must consider where liquidity is held, in which currency and under what access rules.

Money available in one country may not be immediately usable in another. Remittance, taxation, residency, account classification, reporting and institutional procedures may affect access. Currency movement can also change the amount available for a commitment denominated elsewhere.

These matters require current professional guidance. The Liquidity Engine does not provide cross-border instructions. It records the purpose, location, currency, access conditions and relevant professionals.

The goal is to prevent the family from assuming that global net worth equals global liquidity.

Asset-Rich, Time-Poor

Consider an illustrative family with a valuable property portfolio and a profitable closely held company.

A large property payment, university fee and business tax obligation fell within the same quarter. The family expected to meet the commitments through receivables from the business and the sale of a small property.

Both sources were delayed.

The family had sufficient net worth but little accessible capital earmarked for the dates involved. It used short-term borrowing and drew money from an account intended for another purpose. The decisions were workable, but they were made under pressure.

A liquidity review later separated emergency, opportunity and planned-expenditure reserves. It also clarified which company balances could not be treated as personal liquidity and established a calendar for known obligations.

The family did not become wealthier through the exercise. It became less vulnerable to timing.

Liquidity Preserves Choice

Liquidity is sometimes described as unproductive because accessible resources may not pursue maximum growth.

That view is incomplete.

Liquidity provides the ability to wait, negotiate, absorb disruption and act deliberately. It prevents the family from turning a temporary need into a permanent compromise.

Liquidity buys more than time. It preserves choice when circumstances change.

XV

CHAPTER 12: The Legacy Engine: Continuity Beyond the First Generation

A family can transfer assets without transferring order.

Properties, shares, accounts and business interests may eventually pass to heirs. Yet the next generation may receive them without context, documents, decision principles or a clear understanding of responsibility.

The Legacy Engine addresses this gap.

Its purpose is not simply to determine who receives what. It is to prepare ownership, knowledge, authority and family communication so that the financial system can continue when the current decision-maker is no longer performing the role.

Transfer Is Not Continuity

An estate plan may answer important legal questions. A will may record intentions. Nominations and beneficiary designations may assist institutional processes. Business agreements may define rights. These are essential areas for qualified legal and tax professionals.

But legal transfer alone does not ensure continuity.

The heirs may not know which assets exist. They may not understand the purpose of a holding or the obligations connected to it. They may inherit ownership in an entity without knowing the business, the other shareholders or the governance arrangements. They may have access to accounts but no process for making decisions together.

Continuity requires both legal preparation and operational preparation.

The legal documents determine authority and transfer. The operating system helps the family use that authority responsibly.

Ownership, Nomination and Succession

Families frequently treat nomination as a complete succession plan.

The legal effect of a nomination can depend upon the asset, institution and applicable law. Nomination, beneficial entitlement, ownership and inheritance should not be assumed to mean the same thing. The family should obtain current legal advice for its circumstances.

The Legacy Engine records the available facts:

- Legal owner.
- Joint owner, where applicable.
- Nominee or beneficiary recorded with the institution.
- Relevant will or estate document.
- Entity or contractual rights.
- Document location.
- Professional responsible for verification.
- Last review date.

The record is not a legal opinion. It is a map showing where the family requires one.

This is particularly important when assets were acquired over several decades. Ownership may reflect convenience at the time rather than current family intention. A family member may be included or excluded from a record for reasons no one remembers. An entity may own an asset the family informally regards as personal.

Unexamined assumptions are poor succession tools.

Executors, Guardians and Responsible Persons

A legal document may appoint an executor or another responsible person. The family should understand what the role involves and whether the person remains suitable.

Does the person know that he or she has been appointed? Is the individual willing and capable? Does the person know which professionals to contact? Are there conflicts, geographical constraints or age considerations? Is an alternate required?

Guardianship considerations require particular care where minor children or dependants are involved. These decisions should be undertaken with qualified legal advice and sensitive family discussion.

Operational responsibility also matters during temporary incapacity. Who can pay essential expenses, communicate with institutions, manage business approvals and locate records? The legal authority and the practical capability should be considered together.

A family may appoint the right person legally and leave that person operationally unprepared.

Business Succession

For a business family, succession is not one decision.

Ownership, management, income, control and family identity may all be connected to the enterprise.

One child may work in the business while another does not. The founder may wish to retain economic interest while transferring management. The business may depend upon personal guarantees, lender relationships or licences. Family members may expect equal treatment without agreeing on whether equal ownership is appropriate.

These matters require legal, tax, valuation, corporate-governance and business expertise. The Legacy Engine does not prescribe the structure.

It ensures that the family treats succession as a coordinated programme rather than a single document.

The programme may include ownership records, shareholder arrangements, leadership development, delegated authority, continuity of banking, key-person risk, family communication, income expectations and a timetable for transition.

The earlier this conversation begins, the more choices the family retains.

The Family Proof Folder

The family proof folder, or emergency file, is the practical bridge between intention and action.

It may contain or index identity records, asset and liability summaries, important legal documents, insurance records, property papers, business contacts, tax records, digital-access instructions, professional details and immediate obligations.

The folder should not become an insecure collection of passwords and sensitive data. The family should decide what is stored physically, what is encrypted, what is referenced through an index and who may access each category.

The purpose is not to give every family member unrestricted visibility. It is to ensure that a trusted person can identify what exists and begin the correct process during an emergency.

A file that nobody knows about is not an emergency system. A file that everyone can access casually is not secure. Governance balances readiness and confidentiality.

Digital Assets and Digital Life

Modern succession includes more than bank and investment accounts.

Email, cloud storage, domain names, social-media accounts, digital businesses, subscription services, devices, intellectual property and online records may all have financial or operational value.

The family should identify material digital assets, the legal owner, access method, recovery process, service-provider rules and the person responsible.

Password sharing should not be improvised. Institutional and legal procedures may apply. Cybersecurity guidance may be required.

Digital continuity is especially important for founders whose business administration depends upon personal email or devices. The sudden loss of access can interrupt operations even when the underlying assets remain intact.

Communicating Without Creating Anxiety

Some wealth creators avoid legacy discussions because they fear entitlement, conflict or loss of privacy.

These concerns are legitimate. Family communication does not require immediate disclosure of every value or unlimited participation in every decision.

Communication can develop in stages.

Younger family members can first learn financial principles, family history and the responsibilities attached to wealth. Adult children can be introduced to the family's professionals, document system and governance rhythm. Those who will hold formal roles can receive more detailed preparation.

The family should distinguish between information required for continuity and information that can remain private.

The founder should also explain the purpose behind important arrangements. An heir who receives an asset without context may make a decision that appears irrational to the founder but is reasonable given the limited information available.

Legacy planning is partly the transfer of meaning.

Review After Life Changes

Estate and continuity arrangements should not be treated as permanent merely because documents have been signed.

Birth, death, marriage, divorce, relocation, change in residency, business restructuring, acquisition or sale of assets, borrowing, changes in relationships and changes in law may all require review.

The family should establish event triggers and a periodic review date.

Legal and tax professionals should confirm whether documents remain valid and appropriate. Institutions should confirm operational records. The family wealth dashboard should reflect the updated position.

A review should also ask whether the named responsible persons remain willing and capable.

Continuity depends upon current facts, not historical intention.

Assets Without Context

Consider an illustrative founder who had built a profitable services company and accumulated property and financial assets.

His will was current and professionally drafted. The family assumed succession was complete.

During a governance review, the next generation discovered that several assets had been acquired for specific purposes nobody else understood. One property supported a business relationship. An account was maintained for family support. A loan given to a related entity had no simple explanatory record. The founder's personal email contained much of the history.

The legal documents may have transferred ownership successfully. They would not have transferred the operating knowledge required to manage the assets intelligently.

The family created an ownership map, documented the purpose of material arrangements, introduced the next generation to key professionals and established a secure proof folder. Legal questions were referred back to the family's lawyer.

The work did not change the founder's intentions. It made those intentions more capable of surviving his absence.

Prepared Heirs, Not Merely Transferred Assets

Legacy is sometimes discussed as the final stage of wealth. In reality, it is a continuing governance responsibility.

The family should prepare not only documents, but also people. It should prepare access, context, authority, professional relationships and a process for review.

Legacy is not measured only by what reaches the next generation, but by how prepared that generation is to understand and govern it.

XVI

Part IV — Application and Continuity

A framework becomes valuable only when it can operate through geography, change and time. The final chapters apply the model to Global Indian families, establish a review rhythm and help the reader decide whether a dedicated Family CFO function is necessary.

XVII

CHAPTER 13: The NRI and Global Indian Complexity

A Global Indian family can be financially organised within each country and still be disorganised as a family.

An accountant in India may maintain one set of records. A tax professional overseas may maintain another. Banks classify accounts according to local rules. Legal documents are prepared under different systems. Family members hold different citizenships, visas or residency statuses. Assets are valued in several currencies and intended for obligations in more than one country.

Each local arrangement may be correct. The difficulty appears in the connections.

Cross-border wealth requires local expertise in every relevant jurisdiction and a consolidated family-level view linking that expertise.

One Family, Several Legal Realities

Citizenship, immigration status, visa status, domicile and tax residency are not interchangeable concepts.

A person may hold the right to live in one country, remain a citizen of another and be treated as a tax resident according to rules that depend upon days of presence, ties, income or other facts. The classification may change from year to year.

The Family CFO framework should never assume the answer from a label such as NRI, Global Indian, overseas citizen or returning resident. The family should maintain a chronology of relevant facts and obtain current advice from appropriately qualified professionals.

The governance record may include:

- Citizenship and immigration status.
- Countries of residence during relevant periods.
- Travel-day records where required.
- Tax identifiers.
- Primary professional contacts in each jurisdiction.
- Dates on which status changed or may change.
- Matters awaiting formal determination.

This record does not decide residency. It ensures that professionals receive consistent facts.

A family that tells different professionals different versions of its timeline can receive technically sound answers to different factual situations.

The Global Asset and Ownership Map

Cross-border families often organise assets by country.

Indian assets appear in one file. Overseas assets appear in another. Business interests may sit in entity records. The spouse may hold accounts in a third jurisdiction. The family therefore lacks one global ownership map.

The map should identify each material asset, its legal owner, relevant entity, country, currency, institution, purpose, document location, professional contact and last review date.

It should also record liabilities, guarantees and obligations across jurisdictions.

The map is not a substitute for reporting or legal analysis. It helps the family ask the right questions:

Is the ownership accurately reflected in every jurisdiction? Are all required disclosures being made? Does a legal document prepared in one country address assets elsewhere? Who can access the account during an emergency? Does the family understand the currency in which a future obligation must be met?

A consolidated view can reveal that the family is more concentrated than separate country reports suggest. It may also reveal duplicate arrangements, inactive accounts or assets that nobody has included in succession discussions.

Reporting and Disclosure

Cross-border financial life creates overlapping reporting responsibilities.

An asset may be tax-efficient in the country where it is held and still create reporting, taxation or compliance requirements elsewhere. A business interest, foreign account, trust, property or financial product may be classified differently by different systems.

These matters are highly fact-specific and rules change. The family should rely upon appropriately qualified tax and legal professionals in the relevant jurisdictions.

The governance role is to maintain a reporting calendar, document which professional is responsible, record information requests and track completion.

This sounds administrative, but it protects the family from a dangerous assumption: that because an institution accepted a transaction, all reporting implications have been addressed.

Institutions administer their own processes. The family remains responsible for obtaining the professional guidance relevant to its wider position.

Currency as a Family Decision

Currency is often discussed as an investment view. For a Global Indian family, it is also a governance issue.

The family may earn in one currency, spend in another and expect future obligations in a third. Education, retirement, property, family support and business commitments may each have different currency needs.

The family should record the currency of both assets and obligations.

A large balance in one country may not provide certainty for an expense elsewhere. Exchange rates can change, and transferring funds may involve process, tax, reporting or timing considerations.

The Family CFO framework does not forecast currencies or prescribe hedging. It ensures that the family's future obligations are not evaluated only in the currency of its current statements.

Cross-Border Estate and Succession Issues

Succession becomes more complex when assets and heirs are located in different countries.

A will prepared in one jurisdiction may not automatically resolve the administration of assets elsewhere. Terminology, probate processes, matrimonial rights, forced-heirship rules, nomination treatment, tax and legal recognition can differ.

The family should obtain coordinated legal advice rather than assume that one document governs everything.

The governance process may include:

- A jurisdiction-by-jurisdiction asset list.
- A list of existing wills and estate documents.
- The professional who prepared each document.
- Potential conflicts or coordination questions.
- Executors or responsible persons in each location.
- Document storage and access.
- Review triggers following relocation or asset acquisition.

The Family CFO should not interpret the law. The role is to ensure that the family's legal professionals see the global picture and that advice from one jurisdiction is not implemented without considering another.

Accounts, Repatriation and Remittance

Account classification, permitted transactions, remittance and repatriation are areas in which informal assumptions are risky.

A family member may retain an account opened under an earlier status. Funds may be mixed without understanding the consequences. An overseas transfer may be commercially simple and legally or tax-wise more complex. A returning resident may assume that a visa or overseas connection determines the treatment of accounts.

These matters require current professional and institutional guidance.

The governance system should record:

- The account type.
- The holder and operating mandate.
- The status under which it was opened.
- The institution's current records.
- The source and intended use of funds.
- Questions requiring tax, legal or regulatory confirmation.
- The date on which the position was last verified.

The purpose is not to give the family a rulebook. It is to prevent outdated assumptions from becoming operational practice.

Different Family Members, Different Systems

A Global Indian family may contain members living under different legal and financial systems.

Parents remain in India. One child lives in the United States. Another lives in the UAE. The family owns property in India and abroad. Business income arises in one country while future education or retirement expenditure is expected in another.

These family members may have different filing obligations, access arrangements and succession considerations.

The family should decide what information is shared and who is responsible for coordination. Full transparency may not be appropriate in every family, but the absence of any shared view can create serious continuity problems.

At minimum, responsible persons should know that material assets and obligations exist, which professionals are involved and how records can be accessed during an emergency.

A Returning Founder

Consider an illustrative founder who worked in the Gulf for many years, accumulated overseas savings and later returned to India to establish a business.

He retained overseas residency rights, bank relationships and investments. He also reactivated Indian accounts and began receiving business income locally. His spouse remained in India, while one child planned to study overseas.

The family's questions could not be answered through a single label. Immigration rights, physical presence, tax residency, account classification, business income, remittance and succession each required separate professional analysis.

The Family CFO process began by creating a timeline and global map. Accounts were classified by institution and jurisdiction. Income sources and intended uses were recorded. Questions were assigned to the relevant bank, chartered accountant, cross-border tax professional and lawyer. The dashboard showed which conclusions were confirmed and which remained pending.

The coordinator did not determine the founder's legal status. The value lay in ensuring that every professional worked from the same chronology and that no unresolved question disappeared between conversations.

Local Expertise, One Family View

Cross-border complexity cannot be solved by appointing one person who claims to understand every jurisdiction.

The safer model is coordinated expertise.

The family engages qualified professionals in the places where legal, tax, regulatory and investment decisions arise. The Family CFO maintains the consolidated map, organises the facts, tracks the questions and translates specialist outputs into one family decision process.

Global wealth requires local expertise—and one consolidated family-level view connecting it.

XVIII

CHAPTER 14: The Family CFO Review Rhythm

A family can organise its financial life once and still become disorganised again.

Accounts change. Assets are acquired or sold. loans are repaid. Family members relocate. Documents age. Professionals change. Business guarantees are created. Policies are renewed. Decisions are made through conversations that never reach the dashboard.

Without a review rhythm, the system gradually separates from reality.

The Family CFO review rhythm converts organisation from a project into a management discipline.

Review Is Not Constant Monitoring

Families do not need to discuss every financial matter every week.

Excessive monitoring creates noise, encourages short-term reactions and consumes time. The purpose of a review rhythm is to separate routine administration from decisions requiring attention.

A useful system may contain four levels:

- Monthly or exception-based checks.
- Quarterly governance reviews.
- Annual strategic reviews.
- Event-triggered reviews.

The frequency should reflect the family's complexity. A relatively simple household may require less. A business family with cross-border assets and several entities may require more.

The principle is consistency. The family should know when the system will be reviewed and what type of matter belongs at each level.

Monthly and Exception-Based Checks

Monthly checks are primarily administrative.

They may confirm that material cash flows occurred as expected, important payments were made, new accounts or liabilities were recorded, documentation requests were followed up and deadlines for the next month are visible.

The family should not turn this into a full strategic meeting.

Exception-based reporting is often more useful for time-poor decision-makers. Instead of receiving every detail, the family receives only matters outside agreed parameters:

- A payment or renewal that has not been completed.
- A material change in liquidity.
- A new liability or guarantee.
- An unresolved professional action.
- A document nearing expiry.
- An unusual transaction or access concern.

- A change in family or business circumstances requiring review.

The Family CFO's value lies partly in deciding what does not require the family's attention.

The Quarterly Governance Review

The quarterly review is the central operating meeting.

Its purpose is to update the consolidated picture and produce a short decision list.

A concise agenda may include:

- Changes since the previous review New assets, liabilities, entities, accounts, family events, professional relationships and business developments.

- Updated dashboard Material movements, information gaps and areas awaiting verification.

- Liquidity position Emergency, opportunity and planned-expenditure resources, together with upcoming commitments.

- New or changed risks Guarantees, debt, insurance records, business dependency, cybersecurity, health or access issues.

- Upcoming obligations Taxes, education, property payments, renewals, legal deadlines, business funding or major family expenditure.

- Pending professional actions Opinions, filings, documents, confirmations and recommendations that remain open.

- Documentation gaps Missing records, outdated nominations, incomplete ownership information or inaccessible files.

- Decisions required from the family A short list stating the question, available facts, professional input and required authority.

The review should not become a presentation of every figure in the dashboard. The family can examine detail where necessary. The meeting should focus on changes, exceptions and decisions.

Action Owners and Deadlines

Every material action should have one owner.

A meeting note stating "the family will review" is not an assignment. The owner may be a family member, employee, Family CFO or external professional. The person must know what completion means and by when the action is expected.

The action register should include:

- The matter.
- The decision or next step.
- The owner.
- The professional involved.
- The target date.

- Dependencies.
- Current status.
- Evidence of completion.
- The next review date, where relevant.

Actions should remain open until they are completed, cancelled or formally replaced.

A recurring source of financial disorder is the disappearance of old actions from new meeting notes. The review rhythm protects institutional memory by carrying unresolved matters forward.

Escalating Stalled Matters

Some actions remain open because they are genuinely complex. Others remain open because no one wants to make the decision.

The Family CFO should distinguish between delay caused by information and delay caused by avoidance.

A stalled matter may be escalated by clarifying the exact decision, identifying the missing input, setting a revised date or presenting the consequence of continued inaction. The coordinator should not pressure the family into a regulated, legal or financial decision. The role is to ensure that postponement is visible and deliberate.

A useful status system may classify matters as:

- On track.
- Awaiting information.
- Awaiting professional input.
- Awaiting family decision.
- Deferred with reason.
- Completed.
- Closed without action.

This prevents every delay from appearing identical.

The Annual Strategic Review

The annual review examines structure rather than administration.

It may consider whether the family's objectives, ownership, professional network, review process, risk priorities, liquidity needs and succession arrangements remain appropriate.

Questions may include:
Has the family's complexity increased? Are new entities or jurisdictions involved? Has the principal source of wealth changed? Are responsibilities concentrated in one person? Do existing professional arrangements remain suitable? Are compensation and conflicts clear? Have legal or tax changes created matters for specialist review? Does the next generation require greater preparation?

The annual review may also reconcile source records more deeply and confirm that the dashboard remains reliable.

This is not a market-outlook meeting. Market and investment reviews may occur separately with the appropriate professionals. The annual governance review examines the family system.

Event-Triggered Reviews

Certain events should prompt review outside the regular calendar.

These may include:

- Birth, death, marriage or divorce.
- Serious illness or incapacity.
- Relocation or change in residency.
- Business sale, acquisition or restructuring.

- Major borrowing or guarantee.
- Purchase or sale of significant property.
- Change in key professional relationship.
- Receipt of inheritance.
- Material legal dispute.
- Cybersecurity incident.
- A major change in income or household obligation.

The event may affect several engines at once. The review ensures that one visible change is not handled as an isolated transaction.

For example, relocation may affect tax, accounts, currency, insurance, legal documents, property management, family access and future expenditure. A coordinated review identifies the professionals required and tracks the resulting actions.

Family Meetings

A governance review is not only a technical meeting.

It may also be the setting in which spouses align expectations, the next generation receives appropriate context and responsibilities are transferred gradually.

The family should decide who attends which part.

Detailed investment or legal discussions may remain with relevant decision-makers. Broader continuity discussions may involve adult children. Administrative staff may attend only the sections related to execution. Professionals may join for specific questions rather than the entire meeting.

Good meeting design protects confidentiality and avoids overwhelming participants.

The review should end with clear decisions, not merely greater awareness.

A Small Gap Caught Early

Consider an illustrative family whose quarterly review identified that a property loan had been repaid, but the related closure and release records had not been obtained and added to the document register.

The matter appeared minor. No payment was due and the family believed the obligation had ended.

Because the issue was assigned and tracked, the relevant institution and lawyer were contacted. The family obtained the required records and updated the ownership file.

The value of the review was not that a dramatic crisis had been prevented with certainty. It was that a small gap did not remain invisible for another decade.

Governance often works quietly.

From Information to Follow-Through

Families do not need more reports merely because they have more wealth.

They need a rhythm that identifies changes, filters noise, assigns responsibility and brings decisions to completion.

The purpose of a review is not to produce more information. It is to convert information into ownership, decisions and follow-through.

XIX

CHAPTER 15: Do You Need a Family CFO?

A Family CFO should not be adopted as a status symbol.

The relevant question is not whether the family is wealthy enough to deserve one. It is whether the financial complexity has become difficult to govern through existing arrangements.

Some families with substantial net worth remain structurally simple. Others with more modest wealth face businesses, guarantees, cross-border accounts, several decision-makers and incomplete documentation.

Complexity, not prestige, determines the need.

Signs That Coordination Has Become Material

A dedicated Family CFO function may be useful when several of the following conditions exist:

- Multiple entities and ownership structures The family operates through companies, partnerships, LLPs, trusts or other arrangements and lacks one consolidated map.

- Several decision-makers Spouses, siblings, generations or business partners hold different roles and information.

- Cross-border assets or family members Accounts, properties, businesses, tax obligations or heirs span jurisdictions.

- Business and personal finances overlap Household cash flow depends upon business distributions, personal assets support borrowing or guarantees connect the founder to company risk.

- Many professional relationships The family works with accountants, lawyers, bankers, distributors, registered advisers, insurance professionals and overseas specialists but no one maintains the integrated picture.

- Dependence upon one person The founder or one spouse holds most of the financial knowledge, contacts and access.

- Incomplete ownership or documentation visibility The family can estimate net worth but cannot produce a current asset, liability, ownership and document record promptly.

- Frequent unresolved actions Important matters are discussed repeatedly without a named owner or completion date.

- Succession complexity Business ownership, family expectations, estate documents and next-generation preparation require coordination.

- Limited time The family's senior decision-makers cannot personally administer the growing number of relationships and follow-ups.

No single indicator proves the need. The pattern matters.

When the Family May Not Need a Dedicated Role

A separate Family CFO may be unnecessary when the family's affairs are simple, current and accessible.

A small number of accounts, clear ownership, limited liabilities, no cross-border complexity, updated legal documents, a reliable emergency file and one capable family member maintaining a shared system may be sufficient.

The family may also use periodic project support rather than an ongoing arrangement. It could create the dashboard, organise documents and establish a review process, then maintain the system internally.

The objective is not to create dependence upon a coordinator. It is to create dependable governance.

A credible Family CFO should be willing to say when the family does not require a substantial engagement.

Questions to Ask a Prospective Family CFO

The family should begin with scope.

What exactly will the person or firm do? Which records will be maintained? Which reviews will be conducted? Who follows up with professionals? What remains the family's responsibility?

The family should ask how regulatory boundaries are handled.
Is the person a distributor, registered investment adviser, insurance intermediary, accountant, lawyer or holder of another registration in addition to the coordination role? In which capacity is each service provided? How are conflicts disclosed? Who provides regulated recommendations and implementation?

Compensation should be clear.
What fees are paid by the family? Does the provider receive commissions, referral payments or product-related compensation? Are these relationships disclosed? Can the family choose independent professionals?

Data security deserves specific questions.
Where is information stored? Who has access? Are systems encrypted? How are permissions controlled? What happens to the data when the engagement ends? Are third-party vendors involved? Can the family obtain a complete export of its records?

The review process should also be understood.
How often will the family receive updates? What does the dashboard contain? How are urgent matters escalated? How are actions assigned and closed? What evidence shows that the system is current?

Finally, the family should examine professional behaviour.
Does the coordinator acknowledge limits? Is the person comfortable working with existing professionals? Can complex matters be explained without exaggeration? Does the person protect confidentiality and avoid presenting every issue as a sales opportunity?

Red Flags

Certain behaviours should cause caution.

A product-led engagement may be presented as comprehensive governance while most conversations lead to transactions. Product distribution is not inherently improper, but the role and compensation should be clear.

Promises of returns, certainty or universal solutions are inconsistent with the governance model.

Control over assets, passwords or signing authority without strong safeguards should be examined carefully. Convenience should not override security and accountability.

Unclear compensation creates avoidable conflicts.

A provider who refuses to coordinate with the family's accountant, lawyer or other qualified professionals may be building dependence rather than governance.

A coordinator who gives legal, tax, investment or insurance conclusions outside the person's qualifications or registration creates risk.

The Family CFO should organise expertise, not imitate expertise the person does not possess.

Begin With Diagnosis

A family should not begin by purchasing a collection of deliverables.

It should begin with diagnosis.

The initial exercise may include:

- A high-level asset, liability and ownership map.
- A review of document visibility.
- Identification of major professionals and responsibilities.
- A list of open decisions and deadlines.
- A risk and liquidity overview.

- A continuity and emergency-access check.
- A governance scorecard.

The purpose is to determine where complexity actually exists.

One family may need a stronger document system. Another may need cross-border coordination. A third may need business-risk and succession work. The scope should follow the diagnosis.

This approach also allows the family to evaluate the coordinator's judgement before sharing every detail or entering a long engagement.

The Real Test

The need for a Family CFO is not proven by the number of assets. It is revealed by the number of important connections the family cannot see or maintain reliably.

Can the family answer material questions without depending upon one person's memory? Do the professionals work from a common picture? Are actions completed? Can the system continue through illness, relocation or succession? Does the family receive a concise decision list or a stream of disconnected information?

A dedicated coordinator is valuable when the cost of fragmentation exceeds the cost of governance.

The final question is therefore not, "Are we wealthy enough for a Family CFO?"

It is, "Is our financial complexity being actively governed—or merely managed through a collection of disconnected relationships?"

A Private Governance Diagnosis

Families that recognise these conditions may begin with a confidential wealth-governance diagnosis. The purpose should be to map complexity, identify gaps and clarify the work required—not to begin with a product recommendation.

A diagnosis is useful only when it leaves the family with a clearer picture, even if no continuing engagement follows.

A Private Family Wealth Governance Diagnosis

Reading this book may have helped you recognise that the central question is not only how much wealth your family has created, but how clearly that wealth is organised, coordinated and prepared for continuity.

For some families, the next useful step is a structured Family Wealth Governance Diagnosis.

The diagnosis is designed to identify gaps in visibility, ownership records, documentation, liquidity preparedness, risk coordination, professional responsibilities and succession readiness. It does not begin with a financial product or an investment recommendation. It begins with understanding how the family's existing financial arrangements work together.

This may be relevant if your family manages multiple assets, entities, professional relationships, jurisdictions or decision-makers—and no one currently maintains the consolidated view.

To request a private diagnosis, visit:

https://bit.ly/diagnose-your-wealth

Or scan the QR code below.

Diagnose Your Wealth

Conclusion: Wealth. Clarity. Legacy.

Wealth creation is an achievement.

It may represent decades of work, risk, sacrifice, judgement and persistence. A business was built, a career advanced, assets accumulated and opportunities converted into enduring value. Families should not diminish that accomplishment by speaking only about what remains imperfect.

But achievement creates a new responsibility.

The systems that helped one person create wealth may not be sufficient to help a family understand, govern and continue it. The founder can carry complexity through memory for many years. The family cannot rely on that memory forever.

This is the transition at the heart of the Family CFO idea: from founder-held knowledge to family-held continuity.

The transition does not require every family member to know every number. It requires the family to know that reliable information exists, ownership is understood, important documents can be found, professional responsibilities are clear and decisions are reviewed.

It requires the difference between a transaction and a system.

A transaction can be completed. A system must continue operating.

The family may own excellent assets, work with excellent professionals and make intelligent decisions. Yet the whole can remain fragile when information is scattered, responsibilities are informal and unresolved actions live only in someone's inbox.

Governance brings the parts together.

It gives the family a consolidated view without pretending that every matter is simple. It allows specialists to contribute within their proper roles. It distinguishes what is known from what requires verification. It protects access to information while preparing for emergencies. It creates a rhythm through which change becomes visible before it becomes disorder.

The objective is not control for its own sake.

A family should not create reports, meetings and checklists merely to appear sophisticated. Governance is valuable when it reduces unnecessary decision fatigue, saves the founder's attention, improves professional coordination and allows the family to act with greater calm.

The ultimate benefit is freedom from avoidable confusion.

During normal periods, that freedom allows the family to focus on business, work, relationships and purposeful use of wealth. During difficult transitions, it allows the family to respond from a position of preparation rather than reconstruction.

No system can remove uncertainty. Businesses change. markets fluctuate. regulations evolve. Health and family circumstances cannot be predicted completely. Governance does not promise that every decision will succeed.

It promises something more realistic: the family will know why decisions were made, who is responsible, what information is current and how the system should respond when facts change.

That is a form of financial strength not captured by net worth.

The question that began this book was not simply how a family could acquire more. It was how the family could see, coordinate, document and carry forward what had already been created.

The answer lies in stewardship.

Wealth becomes durable when it is not merely owned by a family, but understood, governed and prepared to outlive the person who created it.

Appendix A: The Family Wealth Governance Scorecard

This scorecard is a starting point for family discussion. It is not a financial diagnosis, legal review, investment recommendation or substitute for professional advice.

Complete it with a spouse or other relevant family members. Differences in scores are often more informative than the total. One person may believe a matter is complete while another does not know that the record exists.

Use the following scale:
0 — No, unknown or not established
1 — Partly established, informal or outdated
2 — Yes, documented, current and periodically reviewed

The maximum score is 60.

Core Engine

1. Do we maintain a current consolidated register of our material assets, including ownership and location?
Score: 0 / 1 / 2

2. Do we maintain a current register of liabilities, guarantees and major financial obligations?
Score: 0 / 1 / 2

3. Can we clearly map important assets and liabilities to the individuals or entities that legally hold them?
Score: 0 / 1 / 2

4. Do responsible family members know where essential documents are stored and how authorised access works?
Score: 0 / 1 / 2

5. Do we maintain a dashboard or summary showing material changes, pending decisions, action owners and review dates?
Score: 0 / 1 / 2

Income Engine

6. Do we understand all material family income sources, including whether each source is regular, variable or exceptional?
Score: 0 / 1 / 2

7. Do we maintain an annual view of recurring household costs and large periodic commitments?
Score: 0 / 1 / 2

8. Are business funds and household funds governed through clear policies rather than informal transfers?
Score: 0 / 1 / 2

9. Are material commitments to parents, children, relatives or philanthropy visible and understood by the relevant decision-makers?
Score: 0 / 1 / 2

10. Could the household continue operating if the person who currently manages payments were unavailable?
Score: 0 / 1 / 2

Growth Engine

11. Do our material investment-related decisions have a documented purpose and intended time horizon?
Score: 0 / 1 / 2

12. Can we view our financial assets and major business or property exposures together rather than only institution by institution?
Score: 0 / 1 / 2

13. Do we know which professional is acting in which capacity and how each professional is compensated?
Score: 0 / 1 / 2

14. Do we review long-term decisions using purpose, liquidity, risk, fees, taxation, complexity and changed circumstances—not only recent performance?
Score: 0 / 1 / 2

15. Do we have decision rules that reduce impulsive action based on fear, excitement, social proof or short-term market narratives?
Score: 0 / 1 / 2

Security Engine

16. Do we maintain a current family and business risk register?
Score: 0 / 1 / 2

17. Have material debts, personal guarantees, pledged assets and contingent liabilities been recorded and reviewed?
Score: 0 / 1 / 2

18. Are insurance records consolidated with ownership, nominees, policy status, purpose, important exclusions and claim contacts?
Score: 0 / 1 / 2

19. Could essential family and business functions continue if a key person became unavailable?
Score: 0 / 1 / 2

20. Do we maintain secure digital-access, cybersecurity and fraud-response practices appropriate to our complexity?
Score: 0 / 1 / 2

Liquidity Engine

21. Have we identified emergency, opportunity and planned-expenditure liquidity as separate purposes?
Score: 0 / 1 / 2

22. Do we know which resources are genuinely accessible, within what time and under whose authority?
Score: 0 / 1 / 2

23. Are known large expenditures funded or scheduled before they become urgent?
Score: 0 / 1 / 2

24. Are household liquidity and business liquidity visible separately?
Score: 0 / 1 / 2

25. Do we have a rule for reviewing and replenishing reserves after they are used?
Score: 0 / 1 / 2

Legacy Engine

26. Do we maintain current ownership, nomination and estate-document records for material assets?
Score: 0 / 1 / 2

27. Have succession, nomination and ownership questions been reviewed with appropriately qualified legal and tax professionals where required?
Score: 0 / 1 / 2

28. Do executors, responsible persons or trusted family members know that they have a role and where essential information is located?
Score: 0 / 1 / 2

29. Does the family have a secure emergency file or proof-folder index covering key assets, liabilities, documents and professional contacts?
Score: 0 / 1 / 2

30. Are next-generation family members being prepared gradually for the responsibilities they may inherit?
Score: 0 / 1 / 2

Interpreting the Score

0–15: Fragmented The family may rely heavily on memory, isolated records or individual professionals. Begin with visibility: identify assets, liabilities, ownership, documents, responsibilities and urgent deadlines.

16–30: Developing Several useful practices may exist, but they are likely to be informal, incomplete or dependent upon one person. Focus on converting isolated practices into a maintained system.

31–45: Coordinated The family has meaningful governance foundations. Attention should move to consistency, action tracking, professional coordination, data security and continuity.

46–60: Governed The family appears to have a mature framework. The priority is maintenance, independent verification where required, event-triggered review and preparation for changes in people, entities, jurisdictions and regulation.

How to Use the Result

The score is not a measure of intelligence, wealth or financial success. A high score does not remove legal, market, business, health, cybersecurity or family risk. A low score does not prove that the family has suffered a loss.

The value lies in the discussion.

Review every question scored 0 or 1. Identify whether the matter requires better records, a family decision, an action owner or specialist input. Legal, tax, insurance, securities, cross-border and other regulated matters should be referred to appropriately qualified or licensed professionals.

Repeat the scorecard annually or after a major family, business or jurisdictional change. Track improvement in the quality of the system, not merely the numerical score.

What Should You Do with Your Score?

The value of this scorecard lies less in the final number and more in the questions that produced uncertainty, disagreement or incomplete answers.

Where significant gaps appear, consider discussing them with the relevant family members and appropriately qualified professionals. Families with several interconnected gaps may also benefit from a structured wealth-governance diagnosis that examines the overall system rather than one issue in isolation.

To learn more, visit **https://bit.ly/diagnose-your-wealth** or scan the QR code provided at the end of this book.

Appendix B: The Family Wealth Dashboard Template

A family wealth dashboard is a decision summary, not a substitute for source records, valuations or professional analysis.

The dashboard should allow the family to answer three questions quickly:

1. What has changed?
2. What requires attention?
3. Who is responsible for the next action?

The detailed registers can sit behind the dashboard. The following sections provide a practical structure.

1. Family Members and Key Decision-Makers

Record the names of relevant family members, their broad roles, countries of residence, decision authority and emergency responsibilities.

Why it matters: Family participation, authority and access may differ. Owner: Family CFO or nominated family coordinator. Verification: Legal authority should be confirmed through relevant documents and professionals.

2. Entities and Ownership

List companies, partnerships, LLPs, trusts and other material entities, together with owners, ownership percentages where confirmed, directors or partners, country, purpose and professional contact.

Why it matters: Family assets and obligations may sit within entities rather than personal names. Owner: Coordinator using records supplied by the entity and its professionals. Verification: Corporate, legal and tax professionals should confirm formal status.

3. Assets

Summarise material assets by category, owner, entity, country, institution, purpose, approximate value, information date and document location.

Why it matters: The family needs one global view. Owner: Coordinator, with data owners assigned by asset type. Verification: Values and legal ownership may require specialist confirmation.

4. Liabilities and Guarantees

Record borrower, lender, purpose, outstanding position, repayment terms, security, guarantor, document location and review status.

Why it matters: Guarantees and contingent liabilities can remain invisible until a problem occurs. Owner: Coordinator with the accountant, finance team or lender contact. Verification: Legal consequence and release status require appropriate professional confirmation.

5. Income Sources

List salary, business distributions, rent, professional income and other material inflows. Record owner, frequency, variability, destination account and next expected date.

Why it matters: Income, cash flow and wealth are different. Owner: Household administrator or Family CFO. Verification: Tax and legal treatment should be reviewed separately.

6. Major Annual Obligations

Record education, tax, debt service, property payments, insurance renewals, family support, planned expenditure and other material commitments.

Why it matters: Known expenses should not become artificial emergencies. Owner: Household financial coordinator. Verification: Amounts may be confirmed through source documents and professionals.

7. Insurance and Risk-Cover Records

Summarise policy type, insured person or asset, owner, nominee or beneficiary record, premium status, renewal date, policy location and claim contact.

Why it matters: The existence of a policy is not the same as claim readiness. Owner: Coordinator and licensed insurance professional. Verification: Terms, exclusions and adequacy require policy-specific review.

8. Liquidity Reserves

Show emergency, opportunity and planned-expenditure liquidity by purpose, owner, location, currency, access time and authorised person.

Why it matters: Net worth does not measure immediate access. Owner: Coordinator or treasury responsible person. Verification: Institutional, tax and regulatory considerations may require specialist input.

9. Legal and Estate Documents

List wills, powers of attorney, shareholder agreements, partnership agreements, trust documents and other material records. Include date, jurisdiction, professional, location and review status.

Why it matters: Signed documents can become outdated. Owner: Coordinator. Verification: Only qualified legal professionals should interpret validity or effect.

10. Nomination and Beneficiary Records

Record the institution, asset, owner, nominee or beneficiary shown in available records, date verified and professional follow-up.

Why it matters: Institutional records may not reflect current family intention. Owner: Coordinator and relevant institution. Verification: Nomination should not be assumed to determine final legal entitlement.

11. Professional Contacts

Maintain the name, firm, role, registration or qualification where relevant, contact details, engagement scope and compensation basis.

Why it matters: The family should know who is responsible for what. Owner: Family CFO. Verification: Registrations can be checked with the relevant authority.

12. Renewals and Deadlines

Record upcoming payments, filings, renewals, document expiries, review dates and professional appointments.

Why it matters: Small administrative gaps become expensive when ignored. Owner: Assigned action owner. Verification: Source records and professional calendars.

13. Pending Decisions and Actions

For each item, record the question, required information, decision-maker, action owner, professional involved, target date, dependency and status.

Why it matters: Awareness without follow-through does not create governance. Owner: Named individual or role. Verification: Evidence of completion should be retained.

14. Update and Review Dates

Every dashboard should state:

- Last updated date.
- Data cut-off date.
- Items awaiting verification.
- Prepared by.
- Next quarterly review.
- Next annual review.

Privacy and Cybersecurity

Do not place full passwords, PINs or unrestricted access credentials in an ordinary spreadsheet. Use secure password-management and access protocols. Limit permissions by role. Maintain encrypted backups. Record who can export or edit data. Revoke access promptly when roles change.

The dashboard should help the family navigate its financial life without becoming a single unsecured repository of everything sensitive.

Appendix C: The Family Emergency File Checklist

The emergency file is designed to help a trusted person identify what exists, whom to contact and what requires immediate attention during death, incapacity, hospitalisation, travel disruption, business interruption or another serious event.

It should function as an index and access guide. It should not become an unsecured collection of passwords and confidential data.

Identity and Family Records

- Identity documents and document locations.
- Passports and visa records.
- Marriage and birth records.
- Relevant residency or citizenship records.
- Details of dependants.
- Emergency family contacts.
- Medical information that the family has deliberately chosen to include.

Banking and Financial Accounts

- List of institutions and account types.
- Account holders and operating mandates.
- Relationship-manager or branch contacts.
- Standing instructions and material recurring payments.
- Location of statements and account records.
- Institutional procedures for death or incapacity.

Do not store PINs, one-time passwords or full credentials in plain text.

Assets and Liabilities

- Consolidated asset register.
- Property summary and document locations.
- Business and entity interests.
- Material financial accounts.
- Loans given or receivable.
- Loan and liability register.
- Personal guarantees and pledged assets.
- Lender and professional contacts.

Insurance Records

- Policy list.
- Owner and insured person or asset.
- Nominee or beneficiary records.
- Policy-document location.
- Premium and renewal status.
- Claim helpline and servicing contact.
- Relevant medical, business or asset records required for a claim.

Policy terms and claim requirements should be confirmed with the insurer and appropriately licensed professional.

Business and Entity Records

- Entity list and ownership map.
- Key directors, partners or authorised persons.
- Banking and payment authority.
- Statutory and professional contacts.
- Key contracts and licences.

- Immediate payroll, lender and supplier obligations.
- Business-continuity instructions.
- Location of corporate records.

Legal and Estate Documents

- Wills and date of execution.
- Executor and alternate contact.
- Powers of attorney.
- Guardianship-related documents.
- Shareholder, partnership or succession agreements.
- Trust or other legal documents, where applicable.
- Lawyer's contact details.

The emergency file should identify documents, not interpret them.

Property Records

- Title-document locations.
- Ownership details.
- Loans or encumbrances.
- Property manager, tenant or society contacts.
- Insurance records.
- Taxes, maintenance and utilities.
- Keys and authorised access arrangements.

Tax and Compliance Records

- Tax identifiers.

- Most recent returns and assessment records.
- Countries in which filings may be required.
- Chartered accountant and tax-professional contacts.
- Pending notices, deadlines or information requests.
- Entity-compliance contacts.

Digital Access Instructions

- List of material email accounts and devices.
- Password-manager location and recovery process.
- Multi-factor-authentication recovery arrangements.
- Cloud-storage and encrypted-backup information.
- Domain names and digital-business assets.
- Cybersecurity contact.
- Instructions for disabling compromised devices or accounts.

Do not share passwords casually. Use a reputable password manager, secure recovery method and professional cybersecurity guidance where appropriate.

Professional and Emergency Contacts

- Family doctor and hospital contact.
- Chartered accountant.
- Lawyer.
- Banker.
- Mutual fund distributor or registered investment adviser, where engaged.
- Insurance professional.
- Business finance and senior management contacts.
- Family CFO or coordinator.
- Cybersecurity professional.

- Trusted family members.

Immediate Recurring Obligations

- Household staff and salaries.
- Loan instalments.
- School or university fees.
- Insurance premiums.
- Property payments.
- Medical or caregiving costs.
- Support to parents or dependants.
- Critical business payments.

Dependants and Caregiving

- Names and needs of minor children, elderly parents, persons with disabilities and pets.
- Caregiver contacts.
- Medical schedules.
- Education or residential arrangements.
- Funding instructions that have been documented appropriately.

Storage and Review

Maintain both physical and encrypted digital arrangements where appropriate. Store the index separately from sensitive access credentials. Identify at least one trusted access person and one alternate. Confirm that legal authority matches practical access.

Review the file every six to twelve months and after a major family, business or jurisdictional event.

An emergency file is successful when a trusted person can begin the correct process without bypassing security, law or institutional controls.

Appendix D: Questions To Ask Your Financial Professionals

These questions are intended to improve coordination. They are not a test and do not imply that one professional category is superior to another.

Use only the questions relevant to the engagement.

Chartered Accountant or Tax Professional

- Which family members and entities are included within your current scope?
- Which records do you rely upon, and how frequently should they be updated?
- What upcoming filings, payments or deadlines should appear on our governance calendar?
- Which changes in ownership, residency, business structure or family circumstances should be reported to you immediately?
- Are any assets, liabilities, guarantees or related-party transactions missing from the information you receive?
- Which conclusions require advice from a lawyer, cross-border specialist or another professional?
- Who is responsible for tracking notices, information requests and completion?
- Can we receive a concise annual summary of material tax and compliance matters requiring family attention?

Lawyer or Estate-Planning Professional

- Which assets, entities and jurisdictions were considered when our documents were prepared?
- Do the ownership records provided to you remain current?
- Which life or business events should trigger a legal review?

- How should we understand the difference between ownership, nomination and succession for our circumstances?
- Are our executors, powers of attorney and responsible persons still appropriate?
- Do business agreements and personal estate documents work together?
- Could documents prepared in one jurisdiction conflict with assets or heirs in another?
- Where should originals and certified copies be stored?
- What information should the family provide to responsible persons without compromising confidentiality?
- Which matters require tax, valuation, regulatory or corporate-governance input?

Banker

- What accounts, facilities, lockers, mandates and authorised signatories does the institution record for us?
- Are KYC, contact, residency and nominee records current?
- Which accounts or facilities appear inactive, duplicative or linked to outdated instructions?
- What happens operationally if the principal account holder is incapacitated or deceased?
- Which liabilities, liens, pledges or guarantees remain recorded?
- What documents will be required to release security after repayment?
- Who is responsible for servicing each relationship, and how are escalations handled?
- What information can be exported for our consolidated dashboard?
- Are there limits, access rules or jurisdictional considerations the family should verify with other professionals?

Mutual Fund Distributor or Other Product Distributor

- In what capacity are you acting, and what registrations or licences apply?
- How are you compensated by product providers or the family?
- What disclosures and transaction records will we receive?
- Which part of our financial assets is within your service scope?
- How do you distinguish product information from personalised investment advice?
- How are service requests, nominations, transmission and documentation handled?
- What information do you require to understand the purpose and ownership of a transaction?
- How often will records be reviewed, and who is responsible for updating changes?
- Which questions should be referred to a SEBI Registered Investment Adviser, lawyer, accountant or tax professional?

SEBI Registered Investment Advisor, Where Engaged

- What is your current registration status and permitted scope?
- What services are included in the engagement and what remains outside it?
- How are fees calculated and disclosed?
- What conflicts or related business interests should the family understand?
- What information is required for the suitability and risk-assessment process?
- How are recommendations documented and reviewed?
- Who is responsible for implementation and transaction execution?
- How do you coordinate with our tax, legal, distribution and Family CFO relationships?
- What records will the family receive if the engagement ends?

Insurance Professional

- In what licensed capacity are you acting and how are you compensated?
- What risk was each existing policy intended to address?
- Who owns the policy, who is insured and what nominee or beneficiary is recorded?
- Are premium status, contact details and policy documents current?
- What exclusions, waiting periods, disclosures or conditions require particular attention?
- What documents would be required for a claim?
- Who will assist the family during claim notification and servicing?
- Which policies relate to business risks, loans, key persons or property?
- When should the family review adequacy with an appropriately qualified professional?
- What changes in health, occupation, ownership or family circumstances should be reported?

Business or Corporate-Finance Professional

- Which borrowings, guarantees, pledges and contingent liabilities affect promoters personally?
- Which assets are used by the business but owned elsewhere?
- What payments or approvals depend upon one key person?
- What would happen to working capital if family withdrawals increased or collections slowed?
- Which lender covenants, renewal dates and reporting obligations should appear on the family calendar?
- Is the business dependent upon one customer, supplier, employee, licence or technology?
- Which authority and access arrangements apply during the founder's absence?
- What business-continuity work requires legal, insurance, banking or cybersecurity support?

Family CFO or Wealth-Governance Coordinator

- What is the precise scope of the coordination role?
- Which regulated or specialised services are provided by other professionals?
- What registrations, licences or qualifications do you hold in addition to the coordination role?
- How are fees, commissions, referrals and conflicts disclosed?
- Which information will be collected and where will it be stored?
- Who can access, edit and export the family's data?
- How are decisions, actions, owners and deadlines recorded?
- What does the quarterly review produce?
- How are existing professionals involved?
- How do you respond when a matter falls outside your competence or registration?
- What happens to records and access when the engagement ends?
- How will the family know that the dashboard remains current?

The best professional relationships become stronger when scope, information, responsibility and follow-through are clear.

Appendix E: The 90-Day Family CFO Implementation Roadmap

Ninety days can establish the foundation of a Family Wealth Operating System. It cannot complete every legal, tax, investment, insurance or succession matter.

The objective is to create visibility, identify urgent gaps, assign responsibilities and establish a review rhythm.

Days 1–30: Visibility

Primary objective: Create a dependable map of the family's financial structure.

Core activities

- Identify relevant family members, entities and decision-makers.
- Define the scope of assets, liabilities, countries and businesses to be included.
- Collect existing statements, ownership records, loan documents, insurance records and legal documents.
- Create the initial asset register.
- Create the liability, guarantee and obligation register.
- Map ownership and entities.
- List banks, institutions and professional relationships.
- Record document locations.
- Identify urgent renewals, payments, filings and missing information.
- Establish secure storage, access and data-handling rules.

Expected governance outputs

- Family and decision-maker map.
- Initial asset and liability registers.
- Entity and ownership map.
- Professional contact list.

- Document index.
- Urgent-action list.
- Data-security protocol.

Common mistakes

- Trying to verify every figure before creating the first map.
- Mixing confirmed facts with estimates without labelling them.
- Collecting documents without recording purpose or location.
- Including only financial assets and ignoring businesses, properties, guarantees or obligations.
- Giving unrestricted access to sensitive data for convenience.

Specialist support

Legal ownership, entity records, tax status, account classification and valuation may require lawyers, chartered accountants, institutions and other qualified professionals.

Days 31–60: Risk and Readiness

Primary objective: Identify exposures that could disrupt the family and determine which matters require urgent professional attention.

Core activities

- Prepare a family and business risk register.
- Map death, disability, illness, income and key-person dependencies.
- Review material liabilities, guarantees and pledged assets.
- Consolidate existing insurance records.
- Record policy ownership, nominees, renewal status and claim contacts.
- Identify household and business liquidity requirements.
- Distinguish emergency, opportunity and planned-expenditure needs.
- Create the annual family commitment calendar.
- Identify business-to-family cash-flow dependence.
- Review document, access and succession gaps.

- Begin the emergency-file index.
- Assign every material question to a family member, coordinator or specialist.

Expected governance outputs

- Risk register.
- Insurance-record summary.
- Liquidity-purpose map.
- Annual commitment calendar.
- Business and household dependency map.
- Emergency-file structure.
- Specialist referral list.

Common mistakes

- Treating insurance as the entire risk plan.
- Using generic reserve formulas without examining family obligations.
- Assuming business balances are household liquidity.
- Attempting to interpret legal or policy terms without qualified assistance.
- Identifying risks without assigning an action owner.

Specialist support

Insurance adequacy, legal liability, guarantee status, tax treatment, business continuity, cybersecurity and regulated financial questions require appropriately licensed or qualified professionals.

Days 61–90: Governance

Primary objective: Convert the collected information into an operating and review system.

Core activities

- Create the consolidated family wealth dashboard.
- Identify material changes and unresolved information.
- Establish decision and approval protocols.
- Create the decision log.
- Create the action register with owners and deadlines.
- Coordinate professional inputs around specific family questions.
- Finalise the emergency-file index and access protocol.
- Identify event triggers requiring immediate review.
- Establish monthly or exception-based administration.
- Establish quarterly governance reviews.
- Establish the annual strategic review.
- Prepare the first family governance meeting.
- Record matters deliberately deferred and the reason.

Expected governance outputs

- Family wealth dashboard.
- Decision-authority map.
- Decision log.
- Action register.
- Review calendar.
- Quarterly meeting agenda.
- Exception-reporting process.
- First 12-month governance plan.

Common mistakes

- Designing a dashboard too detailed to maintain.
- Conducting meetings without a decision list.
- Assigning actions to "the family" rather than a named owner.
- Allowing old actions to disappear from later reviews.
- Treating the 90-day project as complete governance.
- Allowing the coordinator to cross professional or regulatory boundaries.

Specialist support

The family's existing professionals should verify matters within their scope and record the resulting actions. Regulated implementation should remain with appropriately authorised persons.

The First Governance Review

At the end of the 90-day period, the family should hold a review focused on decisions rather than data collection.

The meeting should answer:

- What is now visible that was previously unclear?
- Which information remains unverified?
- Which risks require immediate action?
- Which professional matters are open?
- What decisions must the family make?
- Who owns each action?
- What will be reviewed next quarter?
- Which matters should remain confidential and to whom?
- Does the system require ongoing external coordination or can it be maintained internally?

The family should leave with a short action list and a date for the next review.

Ninety days can establish the operating foundation. Governance becomes durable only when the system continues through periodic updates, event-triggered reviews and disciplined follow-through.

Your Next Step Diagnose Your Wealth

As wealth grows, the family's financial life can become divided across assets, businesses, entities, banks, documents, professionals and generations.

A Family Wealth Governance Diagnosis provides a structured view of how these different parts connect.

It may help your family identify:

- Missing or outdated financial records.
- Ownership and documentation gaps.
- Unclear professional responsibilities.
- Liquidity and risk-readiness concerns.
- Unresolved family and business dependencies.
- Succession and continuity issues requiring specialist attention.
- Decisions that remain pending because no one owns the complete picture.

The process begins with understanding—not with selling a product.

Request a Private Conversation

Visit: **https://bit.ly/diagnose-your-wealth**
Website: **www.tandyfinserv.com**
QR code:

Diagnose Your Wealth

TFS Private Wealth

Wealth. Clarity. Legacy.

Victor Tandy is the Founder of Tandy FinServ and a Family CFO. The Family CFO model described in this book is a wealth-governance, coordination, documentation and decision-support framework. Regulated financial activities and specialised legal, tax, estate-planning and other professional services must be undertaken by appropriately registered, licensed or qualified professionals.

ACKNOWLEDGEMENTS

A book may carry one author's name, but it is rarely shaped by one person alone.

The Family CFO has grown from years of conversations with business owners, professionals, affluent families, NRIs and individuals carrying responsibility for both wealth and family. Their questions, concerns and experiences revealed a recurring truth: financial success can create complexity faster than families create systems to manage it.

I am grateful to every client, prospective client and family who trusted me with conversations about their financial lives. Their identities and circumstances remain confidential, but the patterns I observed through these interactions helped shape many of the ideas explored in this book.

My sincere appreciation goes to the chartered accountants, lawyers, bankers, insurance professionals, mutual fund professionals, tax specialists and other experts with whom I have interacted over the years. Their work reinforced an important principle behind this book: no single professional can—or should—replace specialised expertise. The real opportunity lies in helping that expertise work together within a coordinated family-level system.

I also thank my colleagues, associates and professional network at Tandy FinServ and TFS Private Wealth. Their support, discussions and practical insights have contributed to the continuing development of the Family CFO framework.

To my family, thank you for your patience, encouragement and understanding during the many hours spent thinking, writing, reviewing and refining this book. Every meaningful professional pursuit is supported by sacrifices that often remain unseen. I remain deeply grateful for yours.

I am thankful to the authors, researchers, educators and practitioners whose work on family enterprise, governance, succession, stewardship and financial organisation has influenced my understanding over the years.

Their contributions have helped create the broader intellectual foundation within which this book has been written.

Finally, my gratitude goes to you, the reader.

By choosing this book, you have chosen to look beyond products, transactions and isolated decisions. You have chosen to ask how your family's financial life can become more organised, coordinated and prepared for continuity.

That willingness to ask better questions is where meaningful governance begins.

www.ingramcontent.com/pod-product-compliance
Lightning Source LLC
LaVergne TN
LVHW100316210926
848480LV00003B/1145
* 9 7 9 8 9 0 5 8 4 1 5 7 6 *